FINISH LINE

Reading

for the Common Core State Standards

GRADE 2

Continental

Acknowledgments

Illustrations: Page 6: Estella Hickman; Page 8, 9, 10, 13, 14, 22, 23, 25, 32, 36, 37, 38, 39, 41, 55, 67, 69, 76, 83, 84, 116, 129 *grizzly bear,* 142, 148, 152, 153, 154, 165, 170, 183, 197, 204: Laurie Conley; Page 18: Carolyn Williams; Page 24, 38: Jane Yamada; Page 31, 207: Harry Norcross; Page 40, 129 *polar bear:* Matt LeBarre; Page 110, 146: Doris Ettlinger; Page 185: Jim McConnell

Photographs: Page 6: www.istockphoto.com/Daniel Van Beek; Page 26: www.shutterstock.com, Viacheslav V. Fedorov; Page 35: Russell Illig; Page 44: Image used under Creative Commons from Aaron Siirila; Page 58: Library of Congress, Prints and Photographs Division, LC-DIG-ppmsca-19301; Page 61: NOAA's Ark-Animals Collection; Page 88: Kent Knudson/PhotoLink; Page 92: Images used under Creative Commons from Monica Nguyen; Page 95, 102, 179 *cirrus and cumulus,* 218: Royalty-Free/Corbis; Page 104: SW Productions; Page 112: www.shutterstock.com, Sam Chadwick; Page 127: Cybermedia; Page 128: www.photos.com; Page 130: Ryan McVay; Page 131, 137: EyeWire, Inc.; Page 136: www.shutterstock.com, Andresr; Page 144: Library of Congress, Prints and Photographs Division, LC-USZC4-9670; Page 161: Lawrence Jackson; Page 179 *stratus:* NOAA's National Weather Service Collection, Robert F. Kresge; Page 188: Harry Shipler; Page 191: Soakologist; Page 200 *diesel train:* www.railimages.com; Page 200 *maglev train:* Image used under Creative Commons from teepi; Page 207: www.istockphoto.com/Carmen Martínez Banús; Page 209: www.photos.com; Page 217: ©Bettmann/CORBIS

Table of Contents

Welcome to Finish Line Reading for the Common Core State Standards

This book will give you practice in the skills to be an effective reader. It will also help you to get ready for reading tests.

The material in this book is aligned to the Common Core State Standards for English Language Arts and Literacy in History, Social Studies, Science, and Technical Subjects. The Common Core State Standards (CCSS) build on the education standards developed by the states. This book will help you practice the skills necessary to be a literate person in the 21st century.

In the lessons of this book, you will read informational and literary text and then answer multiple-choice and short-response questions about them. The lessons in this book are in three parts:

- The first part introduces the reading skill you are going to study and explains what it is and how you use it.

- The second part is called Guided Practice. You will get more than just practice here; you will get help. You will read a story, poem, or nonfiction article and answer questions about it. After each question, you will find an explanation of the correct answer.

- The third part is called Test Yourself. Here you will read a passage and answer the questions on your own.

When you finish each unit, you will complete a Review Lesson to show what you have learned in that unit. After you have finished all of the lessons and units, you will take a Practice Test at the end of the book.

Now you are ready to begin using this book. Good Luck!

Vocabulary Development

Say you come across a new word. You do not know what it means. You might not even know how to say the word. That is okay! You can sound it out. Then you can use the rest of the sentence to find the meaning. In the next few lessons, you will learn how to use context clues. And you will learn different ways of describing things.

- **In Lesson 1,** you will learn about phonics. You will look at small parts of words. You will see how to sound out groups of letters. Then you will look at longer words. You will see how to sound out those as well. Then, you will look at some words that you should know.

- **In Lesson 2**, you will learn how to find the meaning of words you do not know. You will use the words around the unknown word to find its meaning. You will see how a prefix or suffix can change a word. And you will also take a look at compound words.

- **In Lesson 3,** you will take a closer look at words we use to describe.

Are you ready to get started?

Sounds of Words

RF.2.3

All words are made up of letters. A letter can be either a **consonant** or a **vowel.** Together, consonants and vowels make up all the sounds of words.

Long and Short Vowels

The vowel letters are **a, e, i, o,** and **u.** Vowels can have more than one sound. They may be either **short** vowels or **long** vowels.

Short	Long
cat	tape
wet	Pete
hid	hide
hot	hope
rub	Sue

Do you see a pattern? You usually hear short vowel sounds when there is a consonant sound after the vowel. You usually hear long vowel sounds when there is a silent **e** after the consonant sound.

cape

cap

The letter **y** can sometimes be a vowel, too. It can sound like long **e** or long **i.**

baby	fly

Say these words to yourself. Listen for the long vowel sounds.

able	giant	ruler
became	homework	shiny
beside	kindly	super
between	lazy	student

Vowel Teams

Two vowels together can stand for one sound. They work as a team.

Vowel **digraphs** are two vowels together that stand for one sound. It is usually the long vowel sound of the first letter.

ai	main	**ea**	seat	**ie**	lie	**oe**	Joe
ay	say	**ee**	street	**oa**	soap		

Vowel **diphthongs** are two vowels together that stand for a new sound. The same diphthong may stand for different sounds. Look at **oo, ou,** and **ow** in the chart. **W** is usually a consonant, but it can also be part of a vowel team.

au	sauce	**ew**	chew	**oo**	foot	**ou**	soup
aw	jaw	**oi**	boil	**oo**	boot	**ou**	sound
ei	weigh	**oy**	toy	**oo**	floor	**ow**	grow
						ow	how

Guided Practice

Say each word to yourself. The underlined part of the first word stands for a vowel sound. Circle the letter for the word that has the same vowel sound.

s<u>o</u>ck

    A root

    B joke

    C pots

    D loud

 Listen for the short **o** sound in <u>sock</u>. The word <u>pots</u> has the same short **o** sound. The correct answer is choice C.

l<u>a</u>te

    A pack

    B wait

    C party

    D because

 Listen for the long **a** sound in <u>late</u>. The vowel team **ai** in the word <u>wait</u> has the same sound. The correct answer is choice B.

<u>l</u>oose

    A both

    B wood

    C tooth

    D pillow

There are three ways to say the vowel team **oo**. Say <u>loose</u> to yourself. Only the word <u>tooth</u> has the same sound. The correct answer is choice C.

r<u>oa</u>st

    A bowl

    B outdoor

    C problem

    D somehow

What sound does the vowel team **oa** have in <u>roast</u>? It has the same sound as long **o.** The vowel team **ow** in the word <u>bowl</u> has that sound, too. The correct answer is choice A.

Letters that Change their Sounds _____

Some letters do not always sound the way you expect them to. So certain words do not look the way they sound. You need to watch out for them when you read.

easy	**s** between two vowels often has the sound of **z.**
bread	**ea** sometimes has the sound of short **e.**
none	**o** can have the sound of short **u.**
move	**o** can also have the sound of long **u.**
phone	**ph** often has the sound of **f.**
writer	**wr** often has the sound of **r** alone.
whole	**wh** sometimes has the sound of **h** alone.
whisper	**wh** sometimes has the sound of **w** alone.
ghost	**gh** sometimes has the sound of **g** alone.
rough	**gh** sometimes has the sound of **f.**
right	**gh** after a long vowel sound is often silent.

Guided Practice

m<u>ea</u>dow

   A leaf

   B each

   C after

   D clever

Listen for the short **e** sound in <u>meadow</u>. The words <u>leaf</u> and <u>each</u> have the same vowel team, but not the same sound. <u>Clever</u> has the same short **e** sound as <u>meadow</u>. The correct answer is choice D.

<u>f</u>avor

   A captain

   B whistle

   C photo

   D playground

Listen for the consonant sound **f** in <u>favor</u>. The **ph** in <u>photo</u> makes the same sound. The correct answer is choice C.

<u>wr</u>ong

   A song

   B eight

   C which

   D worried

The **wr** in <u>wrong</u> makes the consonant sound of **r** alone. The **rr** in <u>worried</u> makes the same sound. The correct answer is choice D.

Test Yourself

Say each word to yourself. The underlined part of the first word stands for a vowel or consonant sound. Circle the letter for the word that has the same sound.

1 cl<u>i</u>ck

   A ice

   B pail

   C clock

   D kitchen

2 potat<u>o</u>

   A radio

   B movie

   C proud

   D trouble

3 sm<u>oo</u>th

   A soot

   B once

   C door

   D Tuesday

4 t<u>a</u>ken

   A says

   B carrot

   C parade

   D grandfather

 UNIT 1
Vocabulary Development

5 l<u>ea</u>p

   A cave

   B meant

   C leather

   D believe

6 fr<u>ui</u>t

   A cute

   B noisy

   C shook

   D umbrella

7 <u>wh</u>ale

   A who

   B sweet

   C written

   D shadow

8 <u>Ph</u>ilip

   A pile

   B hospital

   C airplane

   D elephant

9 lightly

   A flag

   B stuff

   C bought

   D together

10 stomach

   A sight

   B chair

   C certain

   D classroom

Word Meanings

RF.2.4, L.2.4, RL.2.4, RI.2.4

Many times you can figure out what a word means by how it is used. This is called using **context clues.** This is when clues in the sentence tell you what a word means. You could ask yourself questions. How is the word used? What part of speech is the word? What helps define the word in the sentence? When you answer these kinds of questions, you get clues to the word's meaning.

Context Clues

Many times you use context clues without even knowing it. We try to figure out new words from how they are used. Look at part of Lewis Carroll's poem "Jabberwocky." Try to figure out what the underlined words mean.

> "And hast thou slain the Jabberwock?
> Come to my arms my beamish boy!
> O frabjous day! Callooh! Callay!"
> He chortled in his joy.

You may not know what the underlined words mean. Lewis Carroll made them up. But what could you guess from the context? We know that the speaker of the poem is happy. The **key word** joy in the last line is a clue. We also see the exclamation points after each word. We can guess that all the underlined words are shouts of joy. We may not know exactly what the words mean. Yet, we have a good idea.

In the poem, we found context clues from the punctuation and key words. This is called **association.** There are other ways that we can find context clues. Look at the chart below.

Type of Clue	Unknown Word	Clue
Similar Words (synonyms)	The hidden camera was **disguised** as a coat button.	The word <u>hidden</u> means almost the same thing as <u>disguised</u>.
Contrast	She thought the fruit was **edible,** but I told her that it went bad.	The word <u>edible</u> is contrasted with "went bad." We know that edible must mean okay to eat.
Description	Our **accountant** is the person who helps us with our taxes.	The word <u>accountant</u> is described within the sentence.
Series	Flu symptoms include fever, cough, and **nausea.**	You may not know exactly what <u>nausea</u> is. But you can guess it is not good.
Cause and Effect	Because walrus pups cannot swim well, they find resting spots on ice **floes.**	You can guess that ice <u>floes</u> are pieces of ice. These would make nice resting spots for the babies.

Guided Practice

Write the word that would best fit the sentence.

Gray squirrels are nearly twice the _____

of red squirrels. *(size, fur, shape)*

> Did you guess <u>size</u>? The clue that helped you would be **association.** The key words here are "nearly twice the." We know that the sentence has something to do with size.

Red and gray squirrels hide in trees because there are

predators on the _____. *(trees, walls,*

ground)

> Did you guess <u>ground</u>? You may not know what <u>predators</u> means. <u>Predators</u> are the animals that will eat squirrels. You could guess that. Just look at the **cause-effect** structure. Squirrels hide from <u>predators</u>. This means that <u>predators</u> cause trouble for them.

At special protection stations, little red squirrels are

_____ shelter, food, and water.

(lifted, made, given)

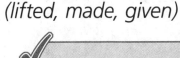

Did you guess <u>given</u>? You may not know what a protection station is. Yet, you can figure it out from the **description.** This is a place where the squirrels get shelter, food, and water.

Multiple-Meaning Words

Sometimes words have more than one meaning. This can be a little tricky. Sometimes you will think of one meaning. However, maybe the context will show you a different meaning. You have to think about all the meanings. Then you can know which one is the right one. Look at the example below.

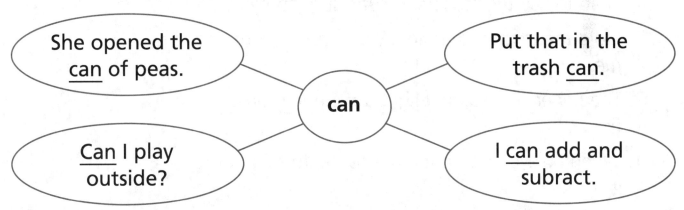

She opened the <u>can</u> of peas.

Put that in the trash <u>can</u>.

can

<u>Can</u> I play outside?

I <u>can</u> add and subtract.

There are many words with multiple meanings. Try to figure out the different meanings of these words: **ball, bat, bit, case, fair, fan, jam, pen,** and **will.** You will have to figure out which meaning is right for the context.

Guided Practice

Set the book on the desk.

    A Read, <u>set</u>, and off we go.

    B She had a <u>set</u> of twin dolls.

    C Do you like my <u>set</u> of clothes?

    D Will you <u>set</u> the cup in the sink?

    Choice A had quick action. Choices B and C had a number of things. Choice D showed how something was being put down. Choice D is the correct answer.

I have a **cut** on my leg.

    A I had to use the scissors to <u>cut</u> out my project.

    B I told the teacher that Jimmy had <u>cut</u> in front of me.

    C The paper slipped, and I got a paper <u>cut</u> on my finger.

    D When I played ball in the house, Mom said "<u>Cut</u> it out."

    Choice A tells how someone used scissors. Choice B tells how Jimmy jumped in front of someone who was in line. Choice D tells about a mom saying to stop playing baseball inside. Only choice C tells how someone has an injury on her body. The correct answer is choice C.

Prefixes, Suffixes, and Roots

You probably read prefixes and suffixes and do not even know it. A **prefix** is added to the beginning of a word. It changes the meaning of a word. A **suffix** is added to the end of the word. Look at the word unfairly. It has a prefix and a suffix. Un- is the prefix. It means "not." The suffix -ly means "in that way."

Look at the charts below and on the next page. You will see some common prefixes and suffixes.

Prefix Chart

Prefix	Meaning	Root for New Word	New Word
dis-	not	covered	discovered
en-	cause to	joy	enjoy
im-	not	possible	impossible
in-	in	side	inside
mis-	wrongly	spell	misspell
pre-	before	view	preview
re-	again, back	turn	return
un-	not	happy	unhappy

Suffix Chart

Suffix	Meaning	Root for New Word	New Word
-able	can be done	like	like<u>able</u>
-ed	past tense	want	want<u>ed</u>
-er	person connected with	teach	teach<u>er</u>
-ful	full of	beauty	beauti<u>ful</u>
-less	without	hope	hope<u>less</u>
-ly	having qualities	friend	friend<u>ly</u>
-s, -es	plural	boy	boy<u>s</u>

UNIT 1 ▚▚▚▚▚▚▚▚▚▚▚▚▚▚▚▚▚▚▚▚▚▚▚▚▚▚▚▚▚▚▚▚▚▚▚▚▚
Vocabulary Development

Guided Practice

They made <u>wishes</u> on a star.   prefix   suffix

Sharon was asked to <u>redo</u> her homework.   prefix   suffix

Mindy made a <u>mistake</u> at the board.   prefix   suffix

 Did you get them all right? The first sentence has a suffix. The other sentences have prefixes.

What words do you know that start or end with the prefixes or suffixes listed? Make a list.

_____

_____

_____

_____

_____

 These are some other words that have these prefixes and suffixes. Do they match your list? *Pre*tend, *im*mobile, *in*side, *en*close, paint*er*, happi*ly*, fear*ful*, comfort*able*.

Compound Words

Compound words are made by joining two words together. Then we get a new word. Many times the words joined together take on new meanings. Take a look at these common compound words in the chart below. You have been using these words for a while. You may not even notice they are compound words.

after	noon	afternoon
eye	brow	eyebrow
fire	works	fireworks
gold	fish	goldfish
bath	room	bathroom
dog	house	doghouse
door	bell	doorbell
rail	road	railroad

Guided Practice

Last fall, I wanted to join the football team. I wanted to be the quarterback. I asked my mom.

"Mom, I have wanted to join the football team since forever," I said.

She raised her eyebrow at me. "That long?" she asked.

"Yes, I play football on the playground with my friends. Now I am ready to play for real," I said.

"I want you to go your bedroom and finish your homework. Then we can talk," Mom said.

I went upstairs and took my homework out of my backpack. When I finished, I rushed downstairs. Mom had taken out Dad's old football jersey. This meant one thing—Yes!

Did you circle all the compound words? Here they are in order: **football, quarterback, football, forever, eyebrow, football, playground, bedroom, homework, upstairs, homework, backpack, downstairs, football.**

Test Yourself

Read the paragraph and answer the questions.

Beluga Whale Saves Diver in China

A diver went into a pool with a whale. Suddenly, the diver had bad muscle cramps. The cramps made the woman <u>paralyzed</u>, as she could not use her hands or feet to move. Mila, the whale, <u>rescued</u> her. Mila pushed the diver upright. The woman could still not move. So Mila used her nose to <u>propel</u> the woman up 20 feet to safety. Mila saved her.

1 Which word means almost the same as <u>rescue</u>?

  A cramp

  B saves

  C safety

  D diving

2 Read this sentence.

> *Mila used her nose to <u>propel</u> the woman up 20 feet to safety.*

Using cause and effect context clues, what does <u>propel</u> mean?

  A to push up

  B to hold down

  C push sideways

  D shake up and down

3 Read this sentence.

The cramps made the woman <u>paralyzed</u>, as she could not use her hands or feet to move.

Using the description context clues, explain what <u>paralyzed</u> means.

_____

_____

_____

_____

4 Which of the following is a compound word from the story?

A safety

B diver

C muscle

D upright

5 The word <u>diver</u> has a suffix. Tell what the suffix is
and how it changes the word.

_____

_____

_____

_____

_____

Read the paragraph and answer the questions.

Copy Cat

I was so mad at my <u>mean</u> sister for taking my
superhero toys into her bedroom again. Why was she
so <u>intrigued</u> by my toys? She even played with them
like I did. She made them fight. I was so <u>frustrated</u>
that I screamed, "Arhhhhhh!" My sister yelled back,
"Arhhhhh!" And before I knew it, our little superheroes
were fighting together playfully. Hey, I guess it can be fun
to have someone who likes the same things as you do.

6 Which sentence uses the word <u>mean</u> as it is used in
the first sentence of the paragraph?

A I do not know what you <u>mean</u>.

B The little boy had a <u>mean</u> face.

C In math we had to find the <u>mean</u>.

D What does that comment <u>mean</u>?

7 Which of the following words is *not* a compound word?

 A bedroom

 B someone

 C screamed

 D superhero

8 Read the sentences from the story.

 Why was she so intrigued by my toys? She even played with them like I did.

 Using context clues, what does intrigued mean?

 A angry

 B hateful

 C disliked

 D interested

9 Read this sentence from the story.

 I was so frustrated that I screamed.

 Using cause and effect context clues, what does frustrated mean?

 A upset

 B happy

 C joyful

 D gloomy

Word Relationships

L.2.5, RL.2.4, RI.2.4

Words are all around us. We use them to talk. We use them to write. We even use them to help us think! We can use real words to describe things. You might say, "The sauce was too spicy." Spicy would tell more about how the sauce tastes. Sometimes we can use words **figuratively** (FIG•yur•a•tiv•lee) to describe things. That means we get playful with language. You might say, "The sauce was like a fire in my mouth." This could also describe the sauce as spicy.

Say you wanted to use a word like spicy. You could look in a thesaurus. This would give you similar words, also called **synonyms.** These are words you might find for spicy—tasty, hot, fresh, and scented. Which one has the same meaning in the sentence? The best choice would be hot. Tasty just makes it sound like the sauce tastes good. Fresh would make it sound like the sauce was newly made. Scented just does not seem to fit this sentence.

Figurative Language

Sometimes you use figurative language. You may not even know it. Many people use figurative language to describe things. You may compare two things that are not alike using the words like or as. This is called a **simile.** For instance, "Her eyes sparkle like the stars." You may **exaggerate.** For instance, "I am so hungry I could eat a horse." Or, you may compare two unlike things without using the words like or as. This is called a **metaphor.** For instance, "It was hailing golf balls."

Guided Practice

Answer the questions.

Look at the sentences in the group. Which one uses language playfully, or figuratively?

    A I popped popcorn on the stove.

    B Popcorn popped like fireworks in the sky.

    C Once I gathered the kernels, I put them in the pan.

    D Mom and I put creamy butter on the cooked popcorn.

Which sentence uses figurative language? Did you guess choice B? It compares the popcorn and fireworks using the word <u>like</u>. It is a simile. It uses language playfully.

Look at the sentences in the group. Which one uses language playfully, or figuratively?

    A Matt walked up to the plate.

    B The pitcher threw Matt the ball.

    C Matt swung his bat with everything.

    D The ball flew like a jet airplane in the sky.

Did you guess choice D? This sentence compares the ball flying to a jet airplane. It uses the language playfully. It is a simile. It compares two unlike things using the word <u>like</u>.

Look at the sentences in the group. Which one uses language playfully, or figuratively?

A Jan's alarm clock went off late.

B Jan got her backpack and hurried.

C Jan ran a hundred miles per hour to school.

D Jane was able to get to school just as the bell rang.

Did you guess choice C? Of course, nobody could run a hundred miles per hour. We know that this is an exaggeration. The writer is using language playfully.

Look at the sentences in the group. Which one uses language playfully, or figuratively?

A Carol slid down the long slide.

B Julie slid down the slide on her belly.

C Julie was a snake slithering down the slide.

D Carol laughed when she saw her friend come down the slide.

Did you guess choice C? This sentence compares Julie coming down the slide on her belly to a snake slithering down the slide. This is using language playfully. A simile uses _like_ or _as_. This does not have _like_ or _as_. We know it is a metaphor.

Uses of Words

We can describe people and things in a few ways. We could describe them with figurative language. Or, we can describe them with **adjectives.** We use adjectives to tell more about people, places, and things. Say you want to describe a friend. What kinds of words might you use? Here are some common words to describe a person.

funny	handsome	loud
pretty	friendly	quiet
nice	polite	gentle
kind	smart	helpful

You probably would not use these kinds of words to describe objects. These words are mostly for people. Say you wanted to describe ice cream. What words might you use for that? You may want to think about your five senses. Look at the chart below.

What does it **look** like?	What does it **feel** like?	What does it **taste** like?	What does it **smell** like?	What does it **sound** like?
white	cold	creamy	sweet	quiet
soft	sticky	sugary	vanilla	soundless

You can also describe places. Say you wanted to tell more about an ocean. You could tell what kind of animals live there. What does it look like? There are whales swimming. There are dolphins jumping. There are jellyfish swaying. These descriptions help us to picture the ocean and its animals.

Guided Practice

Which word would you use to describe a plain potato chip?

    A sour

    B kind

    C salty

    D soft

> We know that a plain potato chip would not be sour. The word <u>kind</u> is used to tell about people. Potato chips would be crunchy, not soft. Choices A, B, and D are incorrect. The correct answer is choice C.

Which word might you use to describe a cousin?

    A nice

    B sugary

    C sour

    D oily

> Most cousins are nice. Choice A is the correct answer. But let us look at the others. Choice B says sugary. You could say someone is sweet. But sugary sounds strange. Saying someone is sour or oily also is a little strange. These are best used for telling about food.

Which word would tell about a forest?

A green

B rough

C friendly

D bitter

Choice A is the correct answer. It would be odd to describe a forest as rough, friendly, or bitter. Choices B, C, and D are incorrect.

Similar Words

There are many words to describe. Yet which word is just the right word? You could look up words in a thesaurus. This would give you a list of similar words, or **synonyms.** Say you want to describe a little ball. You already used the word <u>little</u>. You need another word. These are other words that you might find in a thesaurus—small, tiny, and young. The words <u>small</u> and <u>tiny</u> will fit. <u>Young</u> may not. Look at the following examples. Figure out which word fits and which word does not.

Guided Practice

Which word *best* fits this sentence?

She was so _____ that she could reach the basketball net.

   A tall

   B large

   C big

   D giant

> All the answer choices are close. But there is one that fits best. The correct answer is choice A. Large, big, and giant all tell about size. Only tall tells about height. That is what we are looking for in this sentence.

Which word *best* fits this sentence?

Amir hit the ball with the bat and then he _____ to first base.

   A rode

   B ran

   C moved

   D stretched

> All of these choices involve movement. But only one shows the movement that is used in baseball. Amir ran to first base. Choice B is the correct answer.

Which word *best* fits this sentence?

After soccer, Kyle wanted some _____ water.

- **A** breezy
- **B** chilly
- **C** cool
- **D** calm

Kyle most likely wanted some cool water. Breezy, chilly, and calm also mean cool. They are synonyms. But only <u>cool</u> fits in this sentence. Choice C is the correct answer.

Test Yourself

Answer the questions.

1. Look at the sentences in the group. Which one uses language playfully, or figuratively?

    A The snow was falling down lightly.

    B The snow landed on the roofs of houses.

    C I sled down the snow as fast as a racecar.

    D Mom gave me a red hat and mittens to wear.

2. Look at the sentences in the group. Which one uses language playfully, or figuratively?

    A I unpacked my lunch faster than the others.

    B My mom had made me a cheese sandwich.

    C She also packed me a nice juicy green apple.

    D I was a wolf tearing through my lunch bit by bit.

3. Look at the sentences in the group. Which one uses language playfully, or figuratively?

    A It was raining during our soccer game.

    B We did not mind having to play in the rain.

    C I fell face down in the mud and could barely see.

    D I slipped around like a worm trying to get out of the mud.

4 Which word would you *not* use to describe a hard pretzel?

A brown

B salty

C kind

D crunchy

5 Which might you find on a playground?

A slides

B books

C computers

D radios

6 Which word would you use to describe a ball?

A handsome

B sour

C jagged

D round

7 Which word *best* fits this sentence?

Nina _____ a point when she hit the ball into the goal.

A did

B marked

C scored

D totaled

8 Which word *best* fits this sentence?

Sara's mouth puckered when she tried the ____ lemonade.

A sour

B upset

C angry

D harsh

REVIEW

Vocabulary Development

Read the story. Then answer the questions.

Mystery of the Missing Cat

I am Jonah, a <u>detective</u>. Yes, I am a little young to have such an important job. But it is not as if I get paid to do my work. I do it for fun. I love searching for clues. Today, I have a mystery to solve.

My parents told me that our neighbors have been missing their cat for two days. Our neighbors are <u>pleasant</u> and kind. I want to help them. I grab my notepad and <u>sharpest</u> pencil. I put on my super sleuth detective hat. Then I go to their home.

I ring the doorbell, and Mrs. Nagle answers.

"I am here to solve your <u>mystery</u>. I want to find your cat," I say very <u>eagerly</u>.

"Well that is very <u>helpful</u> of you," Mrs. Nagle says. "Please come in."

"Could you please tell me your cat's name?" I say with a <u>stern</u> face.

I could tell Mrs. Nagle was giggling to herself. Yet, I wanted to take my job seriously.

"His name is Bubbles," she says. I write this down in my notepad.

"When did you see Bubbles last?" I ask her.

"He jumped over the fence into the neighbor's yard two days ago," she says.

I ask Mrs. Nagle to take a walk with me. We walk to our other neighbor's house and ring the doorbell. A cat jumps to the window. It is Mrs. Nagle's cat!

"Bubbles," yells Mrs. Nagle.

Mr. Smith opens the door. "We found Bubbles in our garage this morning. We brought him inside the house. We were just on our way to bring him over."

"Mystery solved!" I cheer.

1 Which *best* tells what a <u>detective</u> would do?

A make mysteries

B solve mysteries

C help a neighbor

D help an animal

2 What is another word for <u>pleasant</u>?

   A bad

   B nice

   C careful

   D horrible

3 As used in paragraph 2, <u>sharpest</u> means _____.

   A most dull

   B most smart

   C most quick

   D most pointy

4 What does the word <u>eagerly</u> describe in paragraph 4?

   A the way Jonah speaks

   B the way Mrs. Nagle speaks

   C the way Jonah rings the bell

   D the way Mrs. Nagle answer the door

5 In paragraph 6, Jonah says he has a <u>stern face</u>. What does the word <u>stern</u> mean?

   A calm

   B joking

   C serious

   D carefree

6 Describe what the word <u>mystery</u> means.

_____

_____

_____

_____

_____

Read the passage. Then answer the questions.

Giant Panda Habitat

by Cindy Lopez

My favorite part of our class trip was the Giant Panda <u>Habitat</u>. It opened in 2006 at the National Zoo. It is made to look and feel like a giant panda's real home in China. The pandas can climb and play. They stay healthy and happy. It lets people study them.

I found out that pandas live in forests in the mountains of China. The <u>climate</u> is just right. The weather never gets too hot or too cold. Pandas eat plants, like <u>bamboo</u>. They like to climb rocks and trees. They like to hide in the forest plants. They like to spend time alone.

Summers in Washington, D.C., are hot and <u>humid</u>. The Giant Panda Habitat is built to keep pandas cool. There are lots of shrubs and trees for shade. The pandas can cool off in the pools and streams. In one place, mist falls to make <u>fog</u>. The fog takes the heat out of the air. In another place, cold water pipes run through the rock walls. This also keeps the pandas cool.

UNIT 1 ▦▦▦▦▦▦▦▦▦▦▦▦▦▦▦▦▦▦▦▦▦▦▦▦▦▦▦▦▦▦▦▦▦
Vocabulary Development

There were four panda dens in the indoor exhibit. I could watch the pandas up close. Only the glass came between me and almost 300 pounds of panda. I could not believe that they were just inches away from me!

I saw the place where food for the pandas is stored. I could not believe how much bamboo those two pandas eat in just one day!

The best part was the Giant Panda Experience Zone. I got to try out the panda yards. I sat on a rock with a panda statue. I walked under the mist. I got to squeeze next to a fake panda in the grotto. I felt a close connection to pandas. It makes me want to do more to help save the giant pandas in our world.

7 In paragraph 2, what does the word climate mean?

   A idea

   B feeling

   C kind of mood

   D type of weather

8 In paragraph 2, what best describes bamboo?

   A a plant

   B an animal

   C a type of food

   D a type of drink

9 In paragraph 3, summers in Washington, D.C., are described as hot and humid. What might humid mean?

    A dry

    B wet

    C cool

    D chilly

10 In paragraph 3, how could you describe what fog is?

_____

_____

_____

_____

11 What does the word exhibit mean in paragraph 4?

    A to hide away from people

    B something on view for people to see

    C a show on a stage for people to watch

    D something that takes place away from people

12 From what you have read, what does the word
habitat mean?

_____

_____

_____

_____

_____

Read the passage. Then answer the questions.

Wrinkled Fingers and Toes

Have you looked at your fingers after taking a
bath? Did the tips of your fingers look like raisins? This
happens to the tips of your toes, too. But why?

We have oil on our skin. The oil blocks water from
entering. And the oil keeps our layers of skin from drying
out. When we sit in a bath, the oil is washed away. So
the outer layer of skin <u>absorbs</u>, or takes in, the water. The
outer layer of skin is covered with old dry skin cells. This
layer is <u>content</u> to take in the water.

When the outer layer takes in water, it <u>expands</u>. This
means it gets larger. But this is too much water for the
inner layer. The inner layer does not want to expand. So
it pulls back. This creates folds in the outer layer. This is
what makes the tips of your fingers look like raisins.

13 What does the word <u>absorbs</u> mean?

   A soaks

   B shows

   C lets out

   D gives off

14 Which word could be replaced with <u>content</u> in paragraph 2?

   A upset

   B careful

   C happy

   D gloomy

15 Explain what the word <u>expands</u> means in paragraph 3. How do you know?

_____

_____

_____

_____

UNIT 1
Vocabulary Development

Key Ideas and Details

Things to read are all around! You can find books that have stories, poems, and plays in them. You read to find out more about the things you like. When you read, there are big **ideas.** These are also called main ideas. Then there are smaller ideas. These are called **details.** Everything you read has main ideas and details. That is what this unit is all about.

- **In Lesson 4,** you will learn how to think about details. This will help you remember what a story is about. You will learn how to pick out details.

- **Lesson 5** is about main ideas. You will learn how to find the main idea of a story. This will help you tell about what you have read.

- **Lesson 6** will help you learn what makes up a story or play. You will learn how to find details about the people in stories. You will think about what happens in the story. You will think where and when a story takes place.

- **Lesson 7** is about finding main ideas and details, too. In this lesson, you will work mostly with nonfiction. You will learn about ideas and events in what you read.

Understanding a Text

RL.2.1, RI.2.1

Vocabulary

aardvark
honest
illustrator
lawyer
president

What do you like about reading? Maybe you like to read **details.** They give more information. They tell about characters. They tell about places. Details tell more about what is happening. In all, they make reading more fun. When you read, think about the details. If you do not understand them, you will probably miss a lot of what the author is telling you. Try to make sense of the details.

Guided Practice

Read the passage. Then answer the questions.

Marc Brown

You may know who Marc Brown is. He writes the *Arthur* books. Arthur is an aardvark. Marc also draws the pictures in his books. He is an illustrator.

Marc was born in 1946 in Pennsylvania. He had many jobs. These jobs included truck driver, cook, and teacher. Then he became a writer.

Marc told bedtime stories to his son. His son liked these stories. This is how he came up with the idea of Arthur. The first book he wrote was *Arthur's Nose.* It was published in 1976. He has created more than 30 books.

Marc knew he must be good at drawing. He knew this when he was only 6 years old. This was because his grandmother kept the drawings he made for her.

aardvark
an animal with a long, pointed nose

illustrator
someone who creates the pictures in a book

"I knew it must be special because she did not save many things," Marc said.

His grandmother helped him in many ways. She helped him pay for art school. She also taught him how to tell good stories. Marc's grandmother was a good storyteller, too.

Marc gets ideas from things that happened to his children. He also remembers what it was like to be a kid.

What job did Marc have before he wrote the *Arthur* books?

A painter

B truck driver

C principal

D salesman

This answer is in the text. Paragraph 2 tells what jobs Marc had. He was a cook, a truck driver, and a teacher. Choices A, C, and D are incorrect. The correct answer is choice B.

What is the character Arthur?

   A a teacher

   B an aardvark

   C a boy

   D a dog

   Choice B is the correct answer. Paragraph 1 tells that Arthur is an aardvark. He is not a teacher, boy, or dog. Choices A, C, and D are incorrect.

Why did Marc think he must be good at drawing pictures?

   A He won an art contest.

   B His mother told him.

   C His son liked his drawings.

   D His grandmother kept his drawings.

   This detail is in paragraph 4. The text says "Marc's grandmother kept his drawings." Choice D is the correct answer. The text does not say he won a contest. It does not mention his mother. Marc's son liked his stories. Choices A, B, and C are incorrect.

Where does Marc get the ideas for his stories?

_____

_____

_____

_____

 Think about what you read. The last paragraph gives us this detail. Here is a sample answer:

> Marc gets his ideas from his childhood. He gets them from the things that happened to his kids. The last paragraph says "Marc gets his ideas from things that happened to his children. He also remembers what it was like to be a kid."

What type of books does Marc Brown write?

A biography

B fiction

C poetry

D history

 You know the answer even though none of these words are in the passage. You must join details that you read with details that you already know. Then you can **infer** the answer. Marc Brown writes stories that are made up. You know they are fiction. Choice B is correct.

Starting Over

I could not believe we had to move—again. I had only been at Forest View Elementary School for two years. I had just made a few friends. I was sad to leave them. I did not want to start over again.

My head hung low as I walked into the kitchen for breakfast. This would be my last breakfast in this house.

"Pick your favorite doughnut from the box," Mom said when she saw me. "The movers will be here any minute. They will need to load the table at some point."

I could feel the tears starting to run down my cheeks. I could not stop them. Saying goodbye was so hard.

"What is wrong, Hillary?" Mom asked as she came over and put her arm around me.

"I do not want to start over at a new school. It is hard to make new friends all the time," I sobbed.

"I know moving is not easy. It is not easy for any of us. Because Dad serves our country in the army, we have to go where they send us. I know you will make many new friends in Texas," Mom said.

"It is just not fair," I said. "No one else has to move every few years."

"Hillary, you know that is not true. Think about all the other kids at your school whose parents are in the military. They have to move, too," Mom reminded me.

Just then, there was a knock on the door. It was my friend, Jenny.

"Guess what?" Jenny yelled as she ran into the kitchen. "My dad is getting sent to Texas, too! We will be moving to the same city you are!"

I got up and threw my arms around Jenny. Maybe starting over would not be so hard if Jenny would be doing it with me!

What is the name of the person telling this story?

A Mom

B Dad

C Jenny

D Hillary

The person telling the story is the main character. You can tell it is not Mom, Dad, or Jenny. The storyteller calls them by name. Look at paragraph 5. Mom says, "What is wrong, Hillary?" The correct answer is choice D.

Why does Hillary have to move?

   A They sold their house.

   B Her mom got a new job.

   C It is the end of the school year.

   D Her dad has to move with the army.

> Paragraph 7 tells why the family is moving. Hillary's dad is in the army. They must move where the army sends him. Choice D is the correct answer.

Which of these is *not* a detail that describes Hillary?

   A Jenny is one of her close friends.

   B She goes to school at Forest View Elementary School.

   C She is happy about moving at the beginning of the story.

   D She has to move because her dad is in the army.

> The story tells us that Hillary is sad about moving. It also tells us that Jenny is her friend. The story says Hillary has been at Forest View for two years. It also says that her dad is in the army. Choice C says that Hillary is happy about moving. This is false. Choice C is the correct answer.

UNIT 2
Key Ideas and Details

Why is Hillary happy that Jenny is moving, too?

_____

_____

_____

✓ **You must make an inference to answer this question. Here is a sample answer:**

Jenny is Hillary's friend. She is moving to the same
place as Hillary. Hillary will not be alone in a new place.
Jenny will be with her. We can infer this will make her happy.

What is Hillary's mom like? What details in the story give
you these clues?

_____

_____

_____

_____

✓ **The story gives us clues about Hillary's mom. Here is a sample answer:**

The story tells what Hillary's mom does. It also tells
what she says. She put her arm around Hillary when she
was crying. She told Hillary she would make new friends.
Hillary's mom is nice. She loves Hillary.

The 16th President: Abraham Lincoln

Abraham Lincoln was born on February 12, 1809. He lived in a log cabin in Kentucky. His family moved to Indiana when he was 8 years old. He lived there with his mother, father, and sister.

His mother, Nancy, died when he was only 10 years old. His father married again. His new wife, Sarah, had three children. She was a good and kind mother.

Abe worked with his father when he was young. He did not go to school very much. However, he did like to read books. He could also do math.

His family moved to Illinois when he was 21 years old. He wanted to start his own life there. He worked on farms. Abe opened his own store. People thought he was honest. One day, he walked six miles to give six cents to a woman that had paid too much in his store.

Abe worked to become a lawyer. He was chosen by the people to help make laws for the state of Illinois. He married Mary Todd and they had four children.

Something great happened when he was 51 years old. He became the president of the United States! He led the country during the Civil War. Abe freed the slaves. He changed history! In 1865, Abe went to a play at Ford's Theater in Washington, D.C. While there, he was shot and killed.

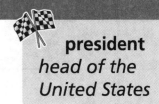

president
head of the United States

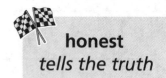

honest
tells the truth

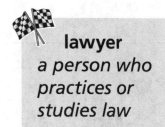

lawyer
a person who practices or studies law

1 Abraham Lincoln was born in _____.

   A Illinois

   B Indiana

   C Kentucky

   D Washington, D.C.

2 Abe was born in _____.

   A 1806

   B 1809

   C 1851

   D 1865

3 Who was Mary Todd?

   A Abraham's wife

   B Abraham's sister

   C Abraham's mother

   D Abraham's stepmother

4 How did Abraham learn if he did not go to school?

_____

_____

_____

_____

5 Why did people believe Abe was honest?

_____

_____

_____

_____

6 What could you infer about how Abe changed history?

_____

_____

_____

_____

Main Idea and Summaries

RL.2.2, RI.2.2

Vocabulary
extinct
hibernation
mammal

Say you tell your teacher you read a book. She asks what it was about. You try to tell her in a few sentences. You probably gave the **main idea.** Telling someone the main idea means you tell what the story is about. This is a key reading skill.

Guided Practice

Read the passage. Then answer the questions.

The Largest Mammal

What is the largest mammal? It is the blue whale! The biggest blue whale found was 110 feet long. It weighed almost 200 tons.

How did the blue whale get its name? The name came from its color. It is a bluish-gray color.

Where do blue whales live? Blue whales live in the oceans around the world. Most migrate, or move, toward warmer water as the seasons change.

mammal
warm-blooded animal that gives birth to live young

What do blue whales eat? They eat krill. Krill are a small shrimplike animal. Blue whales eat about four tons of food each day. That is 8,000 pounds of food!

What are baby blue whales called? Baby blue whales are called calves. Mother blue whales have one baby every two or three years. They are about 20–23 feet in length when they are born. They can weigh 6,000–8,000 pounds. A calf can gain up to 200 pounds a day while nursing.

Why are blue whales in danger? These animals can live 80–90 years or longer. But in the 1960s, they were almost extinct. Humans were hunting them. Today, blue whales are protected. Nobody can kill them.

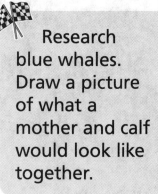

Research blue whales. Draw a picture of what a mother and calf would look like together.

extinct
animal that does not live anymore

What is this article *mainly* about?

A krill

B calves

C blue whales

D blue sharks

The passage talks about krill. It talks about calves. However, these are not what the passage is mostly about. The passage does not talk about blue sharks. Choices A, B, and D are incorrect. The passage is mostly about blue whales. Choice C is the correct answer.

Which sentence *best* expresses the main idea of the first paragraph?

A It is the blue whale!

B It weighed almost 200 tons.

C What is the largest mammal?

D The biggest blue whale found was 110 feet long.

Most times, there is one sentence that tells the main idea of a paragraph. This is the **topic sentence**. In this paragraph, it is the first one. The sentences that come after it tell more details. Choice C is the correct answer.

How do the questions that begin each paragraph help readers?

_____

_____

The questions and answers are one way to write a passage. Here is a sample answer:

The questions tell readers what they will read about. The answers are found in the details.

What is the main idea of paragraph 3?

_____

_____

_____

 Think about what the details tell you. This will help you identify the main idea. The details support this idea.

The main idea of paragraph 3 is where blue whales live. Details tell you that they live in the ocean. They also tell you that they migrate.

Which of these ideas should *not* be in a summary of the passage?

  A Baby blue whales are called calves.

  B Krill are a small shrimplike animal.

  C The blue whale is the largest mammal on Earth.

  D Blue whales eat krill and can eat as much as 4 tons each day.

 A **summary** tells the main ideas. It tells the most important details. Choices A, C, and D are all important details. A summary does not need to tell what krill are. The correct answer is choice B.

Write a summary of the passage.

_____

_____

_____

_____

_____

_____

 Think about of the main idea of each paragraph. Here is a sample answer:

The largest mammal is the blue whale. They can grow as long as 110 feet. They can weigh almost 200 tons. They get their name from their color. Blue whales live in the oceans around the world. They can live 80–90 years. Blue whales eat krill. Baby blue whales are called calves. Mother blue whales have one baby every two or three years. In the 1960s, blue whales were almost extinct. Today, people cannot hunt the whales.

Friends in Need

a fable from India

There was a large group of mice that lived in a forest. They were happy. One day, a group of wild elephants came to live in the forest. Forests have all kinds of creatures—big and small. They usually learn to live together. However, in this forest, there was not enough water.

There was only one stream that still had a little water left. When the elephants ran to the stream to get water, they did not watch where they were going. Many mice were killed. The mice knew something had to be done. However, the mice were so small. How would they get the elephants to listen to them?

The mice made a plan. They sent their leader to talk to the leader of the elephants.

"Sir, I do not think you and your elephants know it, but when you run to get water, you are killing my fellow mice," the mouse said.

"I am sure my elephants do not know what they are doing. I will ask them to take a different path to the stream," the elephant leader said.

"Thank you very much!" the mouse replied.

"It was very brave of you to come to talk with me," the elephant leader said.

"If there is anything we can ever do for you," the mouse said, "we will do it."

The elephant leader laughed at the little mouse. How could little mice ever help the big elephants?

One day, elephant trappers came to the forest. They caught many elephants. The elephant leader did not know what to do. "If only there was someone who could help us," the elephant leaders said as the little mouse ran by.

"You need help?" the mouse asked the elephant leader. "We would be happy to help you!"

That night, all the mice worked to chew through the nets to free the elephants.

"Thank you, mice friends!" the elephant leader said. "I did not know someone so small could help someone so big. I know now that size does not matter in helping others."

Why was it hard for the mice and elephants to live together?

  A The mice were too small.

  B There was not enough water.

  C The elephants ate the mice.

  D The mice did not like the elephants.

This asks about a detail in the story. Look at the first paragraph. The story says that there was not enough water. The correct answer is choice B.

Where do the elephants and mice live?

A at the zoo

B in the river

C in the forest

D on a farm with trappers

This is another detail in the story. The story tells us they lived in a forest. Choice C is the correct answer.

What is the moral of this story?

_____

The main idea of a text is sometimes called its **theme.** The theme is what a story is about. In a fable, the theme is often told as a lesson. It could also be called a "moral." Here is a sample answer:

Size does not matter in how someone can help.

Which sentence *best* summarizes why the elephants needed help?

A The elephants could not find water.

B The elephants were caught by trappers.

C The elephant leader left them for a different forest.

D It was dark and the elephants could not see to get home.

Choice B is the correct answer. The fable tells us, "One day, elephant trappers came to the forest. They caught many elephants. The elephant leader did not know what to do."

Read the poem. Then answer the questions.

Hurt No Living Thing
by Christina Rosetti

1 Hurt no living thing;
2 Ladybird, nor butterfly,
3 Nor moth with dusty wing,
4 Nor cricket chirping cheerily,
5 Nor grasshopper so light of leap,
6 Nor dancing gnat, nor beetle fat,
7 Nor harmless worms that creep.

What is the main idea that the poet expresses in this poem?

A Hurt no living thing

B Nor moth with dusty wing

C Nor grasshopper so light of leap

D Nor harmless worms that creep

The poet tells readers not to hurt living things. She lists them in lines 2–7. Choices B, C, and D are all details or examples. The main idea is also the title of this poem. The correct answer is choice A.

What does the poet mean by "Nor harmless worms that creep" in line 7?

_____

_____

_____

_____

Think about the main idea of the poem. Here is a sample answer:

The poet lists many living things in her poem. She does not want living things to be hurt. Worms creep. People may not like them. However, she says they are harmless and should not be hurt.

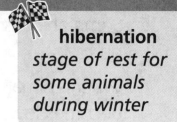

hibernation
stage of rest for some animals during winter

A Deep Sleep

Some animals sleep all winter. This is called hibernation. It is much different than how we sleep. When animals hibernate, they look like they are dead. They do not move. It takes them a long time to wake up and walk when they have been hibernating.

You will notice animals getting ready to hibernate. In the fall season, they will eat more. Then they will hibernate during the winter in caves or burrows. As the animals hibernate, their body will live off their body fat. At the end of the winter, they wake up thinner than in the fall. Yet, they are still as strong as they were in the summer.

Animals hibernate to live through the cold winter. In the winter, it is often hard to find food. It is too cold for animals to live. It is hard for them to run and move.

When animals hibernate, their body temperatures become lower. This helps them require less food because they are not using much energy. Their heartbeat and breathing slow down, too.

Some hibernating animals also store food in their caves or burrows. They will wake up from time to time during the winter to eat a little. Then they will go back to sleep. Their caves or burrows will help keep them safe from their enemies.

Squirrels, chipmunks, and bears are just a few animals that hibernate during the winter. Next fall, look outside your window to see animals getting ready for winter!

1 What is the main idea of this passage?

    A Some animals hibernate to live through winter.

    B Some animals store food in their caves or burrows.

    C When animals hibernate, their body temperature becomes lower.

    D Squirrels, chipmunks, and bears are just a few animals that hibernate during the winter.

2 What is the *most* important supporting idea of this article?

    A Some animals sleep in caves.

    B They wake up thinner than in the fall.

    C As animals hibernate, they will live off their body fat.

    D Some animals wake up and eat from time to time while they hibernate.

3 What is the main idea of paragraph 3?

    A It is too cold for animals to live.

    B It is hard for them to run and move.

    C In the winter, it is often hard to find food.

    D Animals hibernate to live through the cold winter.

4 If paragraph 5 was separate, which of these could be its title?

 A What is Hibernation?

 B What Animals Hibernate?

 C Getting Ready to Hibernate

 D Animals in Caves and Burrows

5 Write a sentence that expresses the main idea of paragraph 1.

_____

_____

_____

_____

6 Write a summary of the article.

_____

_____

_____

_____

Literary Elements

RL.2.3

Vocabulary
astray
directed
dismay
enormous

What do you like about fiction? Is it the people in the story—the **characters?** The characters are the actors in the story. Maybe it is the **plot.** The plot is what happens in the story. It is the order of events. The plot often has a problem to be solved. The plot explains how characters solve the problem. Is it the **setting?** The setting is when and where the story takes place.

All these things make a good story. The characters help move the plot along. The setting helps make the story. No matter how a story is told, it will always include characters, plot, and setting.

Analyzing a Character

Characters make the story real. The author usually describes how the characters talk, look, and act. The "talk" part is called dialogue. You can learn about characters in several ways:

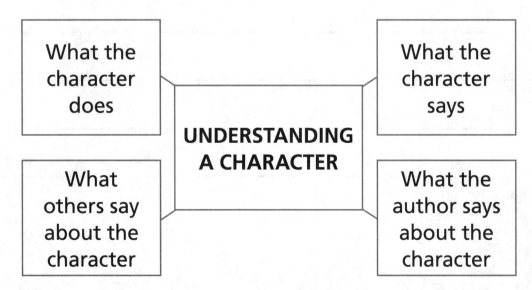

What the character does

What the character says

UNDERSTANDING A CHARACTER

What others say about the character

What the author says about the character

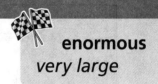

enormous
very large

A Day at the Farm

"Eat your entire breakfast this morning," Mom said. "You will need plenty of energy for your field trip to Edwards' Farm today."

"Why do we have to go to a stinky farm anyways?" I asked Mom.

"It is important to learn where your food comes from!" Mom said.

"It comes from the grocery store," I said jokingly. Mom was not laughing.

"This is exactly the reason why you need to go to the farm. You think farm work is easy," Mom said.

When we arrived at Edwards' Farm, Farmer Dan gave each student a job. Bobby, Juan, and I went with Farmer Dave to milk the cow.

"Susie, would you please gather those two empty buckets over there?" Farmer Dave asked.

"Sure!" I said. "I have never milked a cow before, and I wonder what it will feel like?"

We walked into the enormous red barn, and Farmer Dave brought over one of the cows.

"Susie, you can go first," Farmer Dave said. "Just sit on this chair and squirt into this bucket," Farmer Dave said pointing to the bucket under the cow's utters.

"What do I have to do to get the milk out?" I asked a little frightened.

"Just pull and squeeze," Farmer Dave said as he directed my hand and milk squirted into the bucket.

I pulled and squeezed, but hardly any milk was coming out. "This is hard work for just a little bit of milk," I said.

"You're right, Susie!" Farmer Dave said. "Milking cows and taking care of the animals is hard work. Growing grains and vegetables is even harder. Maybe, you just learned how to appreciate your food more."

"I think I did!" I said as I gave it some thought.

directed
show or explain how to do something

What do we know about Susie from what she says to her mom?

  A She wants to go to the farm.

  B She does not want to go to the farm.

  C She wants to stay home with her mom.

  D She does not want to eat her breakfast.

Susie tells her mom that the farm is stinky. She asks her mom why she has to go. We can guess that she does not want to go to the farm. Choice B is the correct answer.

Which of these *best* describes Farmer Dave?

A mean

B funny

C a good teacher

D does not like children

We can know more about Farmer Dave if we think about what we read about him in the story. Farmer Dave is not mean or funny. He teaches Susie how to milk a cow. Choice C is the correct answer.

Describe the setting and plot in this story.

_____

_____

_____

_____

The setting is where the story takes place. This can include the time of day and the location. The plot is what happens in the story. Here is a sample answer:

Most of the story takes place on a farm. This is the setting. The plot is the story line. Susie does not want to go to the farm. Then she goes and learns how hard farmers work. We can guess she has a new understanding of how food reaches her grocery store.

How does Susie feel when she is milking the cow?

_____

_____

_____

_____

 Read the story carefully. The story gives clues from what Susie says and what she does. We know that milking the cow is a new experience for her.

Susie says she never milked a cow before. Then she says she is frightened. Finally, she says it is hard work for such a little bit of milk. All three of these details show how she feels about milking the cow.

Elements of Drama

A **play** is a story that is acted out. A play is broken into **acts** and **scenes.**

The list of the **characters** in the play is called the **cast.** The characters perform the play's action. The **setting** is when and where the play takes place.

The **dialogue** is the words that the characters say. These words come after the character's name.

Stage directions tell actors how to move around on stage. The directions can also tell them how to speak their lines.

A story can take different forms. Compare this story written as a play to the story on pages 66–67.

Friends in Need

a one-act play

Cast of Characters:

Mouse #1

Elephant King

Mouse #2

Narrator

ACT 1, Scene 1

A forest with many trees, bushes, and lush flowering plants. A small blue river winds through the forest. Mice are running through the forest in search of food and playing with one another.

NARRATOR: There was a large group of mice that lived in a forest. They were very happy. One day, a group of wild elephants came to live in the forest. Forests have all kinds of creatures—big and small. They usually learn to live together. However, in this forest, there was not enough water.

MOUSE #1 *(frightened as he speaks to other mice around him):* There is only one stream left in the forest that still has water running in it. When the elephants run to the stream to get water, they do not watch where they are going. Many mice are being killed.

MOUSE #2: Something has to be done. We are so small. How can we get the elephants to listen to us?

MOUSE #1 *(holding up a sheet of paper and pencil):* Let us make a plan. Then I will go speak to the Elephant King.

NARRATOR: The mice worked the rest of the day on a plan to keep them safe. When it was done, they sent their leader to talk to Elephant King.

MOUSE #1 *(looking up timidly as he speaks to Elephant King):* Sir, I do not think you and your elephants know it, but when you run to get water, you are killing my fellow mice.

ELEPHANT KING: I am sure my elephants do not know what they are doing. I will ask them to take a different path to the stream.

MOUSE #1: Thank you very much!

ELEPHANT KING: It was very brave of you to come to talk with me.

MOUSE #1: If there is anything we can ever do for you, we will do it.

ELEPHANT KING *(laughing loudly as he walks away):* How could little mice ever help us?

ACT 1, Scene 2

The middle of the forest. Mouse #1 is out gathering berries for his family. He passes Elephant King as he returns to his home.

NARRATOR: One day, elephant trappers came to the forest. They caught many elephants in their nets. Elephant King did not know what to do.

ELEPHANT KING *(crying loudly as Mouse #1 runs past him):* If only there was someone who could help us!

MOUSE #1: You need help? We would be happy to help you!

80

UNIT 2 ✖✖✖✖✖✖✖✖✖✖✖✖✖✖✖✖✖✖✖✖✖✖✖✖✖✖✖✖✖✖✖✖✖
Key Ideas and Details

ELEPHANT KING: Yes! Any help would be great!

NARRATOR: That night, all the mice worked to chew through the nets to free the elephants.

ELEPHANT KING: Thank you, mice friends! I did not know someone so small could help someone so big. I know now that size does not matter. A friend in need is a friend, indeed!

Which of these lines from scene 1 is an example of dialogue spoken by Mouse #2?

A MOUSE #2:

B *(laughing loudly as he walks away)*

C There was a large group of mice that lived in a forest.

D How can we get the elephants to listen to us?

You noticed that *italic* type is used for directions (choice B). Regular type is used to show what is spoken (choices C and D). CAPITALS are used for the names of characters (choice A). The Narrator speaks the lines in choice C. The correct answer is choice D. Mouse #2 speaks these lines.

Read the lines of this excerpt.

MOUSE #1 *(looking up timidly as he speaks to Elephant King):* Sir, I do not think you and your elephants know it, but when you run to get water, you are killing my fellow mice.

What do the stage directions in italic tell you?

A Mouse cries as he speaks.

B Mouse speaks with excitement.

C Mouse shyly looks up at Elephant King as he speaks.

D Mouse runs away as he speaks to Elephant King.

The directions tell the actor how he should act. The correct answer is choice C. The directions tell how Mouse should act when he says his lines. He should be *"looking up timidly as he speaks to Elephant King."*

What is an example of a prop used in this play?

_____

_____

A **prop** is an object that is easily moved and used by an actor. Scenery is the larger backgrounds that cannot be moved. A tree or a river is an example of scenery. Here is a sample answer:

Some props used in the play are the sheet of paper and the pencil used by the mouse.

The Story of Johnny Head-in-the-Air

by Heinrich Hoffman

1 As he trudged along to school,
2 It was always Johnny's rule
3 To be looking at the sky
4 And the clouds that floated by;
5 But what just before him lay,
6 In his way,
7 Johnny never thought about;
8 So that everyone cried out,
9 "Look at little Johnny there,
10 Little Johnny Head-in-Air!"

11 Running just in Johnny's way
12 Came a little dog one day;
13 Johnny's eyes were still astray[1]
14 Up on high,
15 In the sky;
16 And he never heard them cry
17 "Johnny, mind, the dog is nigh!"
18 Bump!
19 Dump!
20 Down they fell, with such a thump,
21 Dog and Johnny in a lump!

[1]astray: not looking straight ahead; looking around

22 Once, with head as high as ever,
23 Johnny walked beside the river.
24 Johnny watched the swallows trying
25 Which was cleverest at flying.
26 Oh! what fun!
27 Johnny watched the bright round sun
28 Going in and coming out;
29 This was all he thought about.
30 So he strode on, only think!
31 To the river's very brink,
32 Where the bank was high and steep,
33 And the water very deep;
34 And the fishes, in a row,
35 Stared to see him coming so.

36 One step more! oh! sad to tell!
37 Headlong in poor Johnny fell.
38 And the fishes, in dismay,[2]
39 Wagged their tails and swam away.

40 There lay Johnny on his face,
41 With his nice red writing-case;
42 But, as they were passing by,
43 Two strong men had heard him cry;
44 And, with sticks, these two strong men
45 Hooked poor Johnny out again.

46 Oh! you should have seen him shiver
47 When they pulled him from the river.
48 He was in a sorry plight,
49 Dripping wet, and such a fright!
50 Wet all over, everywhere,
51 Clothes, and arms, and face, and hair:
52 Johnny never will forget
53 What it is to be so wet.

[2]**dismay:** unhappy, or upset

UNIT 2 ☒☒☒☒☒☒☒☒☒☒☒☒☒☒☒☒☒☒☒☒☒☒☒☒☒☒☒☒
Key Ideas and Details

54 And the fishes, one, two, three,
55 Are come back again, you see;
56 Up they came the moment after,
57 To enjoy the fun and laughter.
58 Each popped out his little head,
59 And, to tease poor Johnny, said
60 "Silly little Johnny, look,
61 You have lost your writing-book!"

1 Which word *best* describes Johnny?

   A very angry

   B very smart

   C always joking

   D always dreaming

2 Why do people always try to warn Johnny?

   A He never looks where he is going.

   B He never wants to listen to anyone.

   C He walks around without his glasses.

   D He walks around with his writing book.

3 Explain how the little fish feel about Johnny.

   _____

   _____

   _____

   _____

   _____

4 What was Johnny looking at when he fell into the water?

_____

_____

_____

5 Who saved Johnny from the river?

_____

_____

_____

6 Read these lines again:

Johnny never will forget
What it is to be so wet.

Do you think that Johnny will change in the future?

_____

_____

_____

_____

UNIT 2 ▨▨▨▨▨▨▨▨▨▨▨▨▨▨▨▨▨▨▨▨▨▨▨▨▨▨▨▨▨▨▨▨
Key Ideas and Details

Analyzing Events and Concepts

RI.2.3

Vocabulary
kernels
settlers
storm surge

Ideas, events, and people are often connected. Ideas can make people act a certain way. People can make events happen. Events can also make people act a certain way.

Here is an example. Many people came to America from Ireland. An event in Ireland caused many people to leave. They left because there was no food. The potato crop had failed. There was little food for the people. This caused many people to leave their country. Many of them came to America to live.

As you read, think about the order in which events happen. Also, think about why certain events happen. You may want help understanding why things happen. You can ask yourself, "Why did that happen?" to find the cause of an event. You can ask "What happened because of this?" to find the effect.

There are clue words to help you. Clue words for cause are *if, because,* and *since.* Clue words for effect are *then, so,* and *as a result.*

Look for connections when you read. This will help you better understand what you are reading.

The History of Corn

by Stacy Rummel

The Native Americans grew corn long ago. When Christopher Columbus came to the New World, he saw the corn. He traded with the Native Americans for corn. Columbus brought the corn back to Spain. From there, it was taken to Europe and the rest of the world.

Early settlers to America learned how to grow corn. The Native Americans showed them how to plant kernels of corn with a small fish. The fish helped the corn grow better. If it were not for them showing the settlers how to grow corn, the settlers may have died.

What did the settlers do with the corn? The Native Americans showed them many things to make with the corn. They learned to pound it into meal. It was used to make corn bread, soup, and syrup. Settlers also used corn as money. They traded corn for meat and furs.

The settlers ate corn at their first Thanksgiving in 1620. Corn is still very well liked today. It is the largest crop grown today in the United States. The state of Iowa grows the most corn!

When was the last time you ate corn?

Christopher Columbus was an explorer who discovered the New World.

settlers
people who settle in an area; colonists

kernels
the part of the corn cob that is eaten

Sequence of Events Chart

First	Christopher Columbus came to the New World and saw corn.
Second	Columbus traded with the Native Americans for corn.
Third	Columbus brought corn back to Spain. Then it was taken to Europe and the rest of the world.
Fourth	Native Americans showed early settlers how to grow corn. They planted kernels with a small fish.
Last	The Indians showed the settlers how to make things with corn. They traded corn for meat and furs.

Who were the first people to grow corn?

A Americans

B Native Americans

C people from Iowa

D Christopher Columbus

This detail can be found in the text. It is in paragraph 1. The text says, "The Native Americans grew corn long ago." Choice B is the correct answer.

According to the passage, which of these events happened *first?*

A Christopher Columbus traded the Native Americans for corn.

B Christopher Columbus brought corn back to Spain.

C The Native Americans showed settlers how to ground corn and make corn meal.

D The Native Americans showed settlers how to grow corn and make many things from it.

> Knowing the order of events is key. The passage is written in the order the events happened. Look back at the text. Use the chart for help. Choice A is the correct answer.

What did the settlers learn to do with corn?

_____

_____

_____

> This question asks you to find the cause and effect. The effect was that the settlers learned to use corn. The cause was that the Native Americans taught the settlers about corn. Here is a sample answer:

The Native Americans showed them how to pound corn into meal. It was used to make corn bread and soup. They also used corn as money.

Why were kernels of corn used as money?

_____

_____

_____

_____

 This is a question in which you must draw a conclusion. To answer this question, think about what you know about money. Put that together with what you learn in the text. Here is a sample answer:

Many people liked corn. It was used to make many things. People could pay for things they bought with the kernels. This is because kernels were worth something. They were important. They could trade corn like we use money today.

Caramel Corn

7 quarts plain popped popcorn

2 cups brown sugar

$\frac{1}{2}$ cup light corn syrup

1 teaspoon salt

1 cup margarine

$\frac{1}{2}$ teaspoon baking soda

1 teaspoon vanilla extract

1. Place the popcorn into two greased baking pans. Set aside.

2. Preheat the oven to 250° F. Combine the brown sugar, corn syrup, margarine, and salt in a saucepan. Bring to a boil. Keep on stove 5 minutes while stirring constantly.

3. Remove saucepan from heat. Stir in baking soda and vanilla. The mixture will be light and foamy. Immediately pour over the popcorn in the pans and stir.

4. Bake for 1 hour. But stir every 15 minutes.

5. Line the countertop with waxed paper. Pour the corn out on to the waxed paper and separate the pieces. Allow to cool before eating.

Which of these steps do you do *first?*

    A Preheat oven to 250° F.

    B Remove saucepan from heat.

    C Stir in the baking soda and vanilla.

    D Place the popcorn into baking pans.

> You must follow steps when you bake. Each step has a relationship to the next. If you miss a step or do them out of order, you could end up with food that is no good. Reread the recipe carefully. You will see that choices A, B, and C are all steps that come after choice D. Choice D is the correct answer.

Which of these steps do you do right *before* you bring the ingredients to a boil?

    A Pour the corn out on to the waxed paper.

    B Pour over the popcorn in the pans, and stir to coat.

    C Combine the brown sugar, corn syrup, margarine, and salt in a saucepan.

    D Remove from the heat, and stir in the baking soda and vanilla.

> This question asks you to follow steps in order. Choice C is the correct answer. Choices A, B, and D are steps that come after choice C.

What could happen if you didn't do step 1?

_____

_____

 This question asks you to make a good guess, or a **prediction.** When you make this recipe, you need popcorn. Here is a sample answer:

When the caramel mixture was ready, there would be no popcorn to pour it on. You have to pop the popcorn first.

Consider both this recipe and the passage on corn. Why do you think people began to make popcorn and caramel popcorn?

_____

_____

 You have to think about the recipe and the passage. The Indians taught the settlers how to make many things with corn. Here is a sample answer:

People wanted to try new things with the corn. They made popcorn. Then they made different kinds of popcorn.

Test Yourself

Read the passage. Then answer the questions.

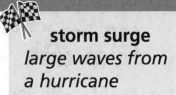

Hurricane!

Hurricanes are storms that are made over warm ocean water. A hurricane can be as big as 600 miles wide. They can last for more than a week.

Hurricanes move around a center, or an "eye." Their winds move at 74–200 miles per hour. On land, they bring rain, wind, and large waves. The waves can knock down houses and trees. They are called a storm surge. People must not go to the beach during a hurricane.

Computers can help tell how a hurricane will hurt the land. They are called Slosh Models. They use the strength of the storm, the slope of the ocean floor, and the shape of the land. They can tell how much harm the storm will cause.

Did you know that hurricanes have names? There are six name lists. A different one is used each year. If a hurricane is very bad, its name is taken off the list. A new one is put in its place.

1 How fast can hurricane winds move?

   A 0–74 miles per hour

   B 74–200 miles per hour

   C 100–200 miles per hour

   D 150–300 miles per hour

2 A hurricane forms over _____.

   A streams

   B ocean water

   C narrow streets

   D buildings that line the street

3 Because of the storm surges, people must not _____ during a hurricane.

   A go to the beach

   B make a phone call

   C listen to the radio

   D watch the television

4 What is a hurricane? What happens during a hurricane?

_____

_____

_____

_____

5 What is used to tell how a storm surge will affect the land? How does it work?

_____

_____

_____

_____

REVIEW

Key Ideas and Details

Vocabulary
customers
exercise
startled

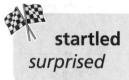

startled
surprised

Read the passage. Then answer the questions.

A Helping Hand

"What do you think you will get for your birthday?" my friend Neal asked me.

"I do not know yet," I answered and threw the baseball back. "It is hard to think of something when I already have toys. I saw a story on the evening news that told about a family that does not have money to buy groceries."

"That is not your problem!" Neal replied.

"Neal, that is a horrible thing to say!" I said, angry at my best friend. "You do not even know why they cannot afford to buy food."

"I try not to think about those things," Neal said as he threw the ball back. "See you tomorrow at practice," Neal said as he left to walk home.

"What are you thinking about, Mark?" Mom asked me later that day as I stared off into space.

"You know that family we saw on the news—the ones that did not have money to buy groceries?" I said.

"Yes, I remember," Mom said. "It is very sad."

"I think we can help them," I explained.

"You do?" Mom asked.

"They need help, and we can help them," I began. "My birthday is almost here, and instead of getting lots of presents, I would like to ask for money for my gift. Then, we can go to the store, and I can buy the family food. Do you think we can find out where they live?"

Mom looked startled. "Wow, Mark, that is very nice of you. Are you sure this is what you want to do?" Mom asked.

"You always tell Maddie and me we should help others, so that is what I want to do!"

"Okay, honey. Let me try and call the news station to see if they can put us in contact with the family," Mom said.

"Thanks, Mom! You are the best," I said as I gave her a hug.

Mom squeezed me back. "I am really proud of you, Mark. This is a very kind and caring thing you are doing for the family."

1 What is the theme of this story?

   A It is good to help others in need.

   B A friend in need is a friend indeed.

   C Presents are fun to give and receive.

   D Friends need to help each other out.

2 Neal is Mark's _____.

   A brother

   B cousin

   C friend

   D coach

3 Which of these words does *not* describe Mark?

   A kind

   B mean

   C caring

   D helpful

4 Why did Mark's mom ask him what he was thinking about?

   A Mark was staring off into space.

   B She was worried that he was not eating his dinner.

   C Mark did not answer her question and she thought he could not hear her.

   D He had a tough day at school, and she wanted to hear about what was bothering him.

5 What does Mark want for his birthday?

   A toys for himself

   B food for his friend

   C money to buy toys for a family

   D money to buy food for a family

6 How did Mark *most* likely feel after Neal said, "That is not your problem!"?

　A angry

　B happy

　C excited

　D worried

7 Which of these details does *not* belong in a summary of the story?

　A Mark's birthday was near.

　B The news said a family could not afford groceries.

　C Mark wanted to use his birthday money to buy food for a family.

　D Mark and Neal were throwing the baseball in the yard.

Read the passage. Then answer the questions.

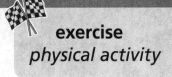

exercise
physical activity

Staying Healthy

Did you know there are a few things you can do to stay healthy? Read on to see if you are doing them!

One of the most important things you can do is wash your hands with soap and water. You should wash for at least 20 seconds. It might help to sing a short song. When you are done singing, you are done washing. Wash your hands before you eat and after you use the bathroom. Also, wash them after you play at the playground.

Besides washing your hands, you need to eat well. This starts with knowing what foods are good for you. If you have a snack time at school, bring a healthy snack—a fruit or vegetable. Learn more about eating well by reading books about it. Study the food pyramid to make sure you are eating the right kinds of foods.

Finally, to stay healthy you need to exercise! How many days a week do you go to the gym at school? You can get exercise in all kinds of ways. You can just play! So get outside and chase a ball! If the weather is bad, think of something you can do inside. You can play jumping games. You can do floor stretches. Do anything to get your body moving!

Add these things into your day. You will feel good, stay fit, and be healthy!

8 You should wash your hands _____.

A for 20 minutes

B for 20 seconds

C until your hands are wet

D until you finish singing a long song

9 Which of these is the main idea of this passage?

  A to exercise

  B to eat right

  C to wash your hands

  D to stay healthy and fit

10 Which of the following is *not* a way to get healthy?

  A jump rope

  B wash hands

  C do floor exercises

  D sit and watch movies

11 According to the author, what are the three things you can do to stay healthy?

_____

_____

_____

_____

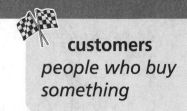

How to Start a Lemonade Stand

In summer, it is blazing hot outside. You would like to make some money. How about starting a lemonade stand?

1. To get started, you will need an adult to help. Supplies you will need:
   - lemonade
   - pitchers (1 clear)
   - ice and coolers
   - signs
   - table and chairs
   - tablecloth
   - paper cups and napkins
   - money to make change
   - money box
   - trash bag

2. Make a plan. You will need money to get started. How much will you need to charge for each cup of lemonade to make money?

3. Choose a place, day, and time where there are lots of thirsty people.

4. Make a big sign. Write "Lemonade for Sale" and the price on it. Make some small signs.

5. Let your friends and family know about your lemonade stand. People need to know where and when you will be open for business.

6. Make your lemonade. Make sure it tastes good. Keep it very cold.

Lemonade Recipe

Juice of 6 lemons (remove pits)

Mix with $1\frac{1}{2}$ cups of sugar.

Add 2 quarts of water and ice.

Float lemon slices in the pitcher.

Add ice and keep cold.

Makes 1 gallon

7. Set up your table and chairs. Hang up your signs. Set out the paper cups and napkins. Keep everything very clean and neat.

8. Have lots of quarters and one dollar bills in your cash box. Use it to make change. Keep it in a safe place.

9. Put extra ice and lemonade in coolers under the table. Fill a clear pitcher with ice, lemonade, and cut lemons. Set it out for customers to see.

10. Smile and wait for customers. Be polite. Make your customers want to buy more lemonade.

12 Which of the following is the *first* step you should take in starting a lemonade stand?

A Make a plan.

B Make a sign.

C Make lemonade.

D Make a nice table.

13 In step 9, why does the author *most* likely want you to use a clear pitcher?

 A so the ice will not melt

 B so customers can see it better

 C so you can see if it needs ice

 D so the lemons do not turn brown

14 What should you write on your sign?

 A We want lemonade.

 B Lemonade for sale.

 C Do you want lemonade?

 D Do you want something to drink?

15 What is the main point of step 6?

 A to give a list of supplies

 B to explain how the ice works

 C to show how to pour drinks

 D to tell how to make lemonade

Craft and Structure

Writers are builders. Words are their building blocks. Writers build poems with words, lines, and stanzas. Writers also build stories and nonfiction. They do this with words, sentences, and chapters.

● **In Lesson 8,** you will learn how writers choose words with care. You will learn about structure in poems and stories. Stories all have a beginning, middle, and end. You will learn how stories are put together to make meaning.

● **In Lesson 9,** you will learn about text features in nonfiction. You will learn to find these features and how to use them.

● **In Lesson 10,** you will learn about point of view and purpose. The point of view shapes what you read. The author's purpose is why the author is writing.

Literary Structure

RL.2.4, RL.2.5

Vocabulary
alliteration
onomatopoeia
stanzas

Everything you read has a structure. A book has paragraphs and chapters. A play has acts and scenes. The author uses these smaller structures to build upon. This is how the author creates an image or idea. It is also how the author keeps you reading to find out what happens next.

Poems

stanza
a group of lines in a poem

A poem is made of words, lines, and stanzas. **Stanzas,** or verses, are groups of lines broken up by spaces. These are the building blocks of a poem.

The author picks words carefully. The sounds of words are important. The author may use words that **rhyme.** These words have the same ending sounds, like *cake, make,* and *snake.* Sometimes these rhyming words come at the end of lines.

> *As I was going up the stair*
> *I met a man who wasn't there.*

Sometimes these rhyming words appear in the same line:

> *There was a little **boy** who had a **toy***

The author may repeat some words or lines in a poem.

> **Mary, Mary,** *quite contrary.*
> *How does your garden grow*

Poems sometimes have words that begin with the same consonant sound. This is called **alliteration.**

> **He hummed as he hunted for honeybees.**

alliteration
repeated beginning sounds of words

Some words sound like what they mean. This is called **onomatopoeia** (ah•no•mat•uh•PEE•uh). Some examples are *gurgling, hissing, whoosh,* and *clank.*

onomatopoeia
words that sound like what they mean

Just like music, poems have a beat or **rhythm.** They have a pattern of stressed and unstressed beats. Stressed beats are said with more force. Stresses usually come every other beat. You can clap the rhythm of a poem.

> *Star* **light,** *star* **bright,**
> *The first* **star** *I* **see** *to***night,**

Guided Practice

Once I Saw a Little Bird

1 Once I saw a little bird
2 Come hop, hop, hop,
3 And I cried, "Little bird,
4 Will you stop, stop, stop?"

5 I was going to the window
6 To say, "How do you do?"
7 But he shook his little tail
8 And far away he flew.

How many lines are in each stanza?

A one

B two

C three

D four

 There are two stanzas, or verses, in this poem. Each stanza has four lines. Choice D is the correct answer.

In stanza 2, what happens after the child asks "How do you do"?

A The bird flies away.

B The bird keeps hopping.

C The bird stays near the window.

D The bird sings a song back to the child.

Look again at lines 5–8. The bird shakes his tail and flies away. Since "shakes his tail" is not a choice, the correct answer is choice A.

Why does the speaker repeat the words <u>hop</u> and <u>stop</u> in lines 2 and 4?

A to show anger

B to show sadness

C to show boredom

D to show excitement

<u>Hop</u> and <u>stop</u> rhyme. They also are repeated in the lines. The words are action words. They get the reader excited. The best answer is choice D.

Read this line from stanza 2.

But he shook his little tail

How many beats of rhythm do you count?

A two

B three

C four

D five

You can clap the beats of each line in a poem. For this poem, you start with a stressed beat on the first word. Read this line and clap on these syllables: *but, shook, lit-* and *tail.* We clap four times. We say that there are four beats. The correct answer is choice C.

Read the poem. Then answer the questions.

Horsey, Horsey

1 Horsey, horsey, don't you stop

2 Just let your feet go clippety clop,

3 The tail goes swish and the wheels go 'round,

4 Giddy, up, we are homeward bound.

Read this line from the poem.

Just let your feet go clippety clop

The words clippety clop are examples of _____.

   A onomatopoeia

   B rhythm

   C rhyme

   D stanzas

   The speaker can hear the horse's feet go clippety clop. This means we can hear the sounds that something makes. Clippety clop sounds like what it means. Rhythm is the pattern of beats. Rhyme is words that have the same sending sounds. Stanzas are the groups of lines in a poem. Choices B, C, and D are incorrect. The correct answer is choice A.

What other word from the poem is an example of onomatopoeia?

_____

_____

_____

   Look for a word that sounds like what it means. Here is a sample answer:

   In line 3, the poet writes, "The tail goes swish and the wheels go 'round." The tail that goes swish makes a noise. This is an example of onomatopoeia.

Which lines of the poem rhyme?

A lines 1 and 2

B lines 1 and 3

C lines 1 and 4

D lines 2 and 3

In this poem, lines 1 and 2 rhyme. Lines 3 and 4 also rhyme. We would call this an AABB rhyme pattern. The As stand for the -*op* sound. And the Bs stand for the -*ound* sound.

Which sound is repeated in line 2?

_____

_____

This question asks you about alliteration. This is when poets often repeat the same beginning sounds.

In line 2, the author repeats the beginning sound /cl/. The words are clippety and clop.

UNIT 3
Craft and Structure

Which line has a word that is repeated?

A line 1

B line 2

C line 2

D line 4

 In line 1, the poet repeats the word <u>horsey</u>. The correct answer is choice A.

Stories

Stories have structure, too. They have a beginning, middle, and end. In the beginning of a story, you usually meet the characters. You also learn about the setting. It also tells about a **conflict.** This is a problem in the story. The middle tells what happens. It tells how the characters try to solve the problem. The end tells how the problem is solved.

Guided Practice

Read the story. Then answer the questions.

The Cat and the Mouse

an adaptation

Cat and Mouse were playing in a barn. Suddenly, Cat bit off Mouse's tail. "Please, Puss, give me back my tail!" cried Mouse.

"No," said Cat, "I will not give back your tail until you go to Cow to get me some milk."

Mouse ran to Cow. "Please, Cow, give me some milk for Cat so she will give me back my tail."

"No," said Cow, "I will not give you milk until you go to Farmer to get me some hay."

Mouse ran to Farmer. "Please, Farmer, give me some hay for Cow so she will give me some milk for Cat, so she will give me back my tail."

"No," said Farmer, "I will give you no hay until you go to Baker to get me some bread."

Mouse ran to Baker. "Please, Baker, give me some bread for Farmer, so he will give me some hay for Cow, so she will give me some milk for Cat, so she will give me back my tail."

"Well," said Baker, "I will give you some bread, but do not eat my flour, or I will cut off your head!" Baker gave Mouse bread which she took to Farmer. Farmer gave Mouse hay which she took to Cow. Cow gave Mouse milk which she took to Cat. Then Cat gave back Mouse's tail.

What text structure did the author use in this story?

A acts and scenes

B lines and stanzas

C paragraphs and chapters

D beginning, middle, and end

This passage is not a play. There are no acts and scenes. It is not a poem. There are no lines and stanzas. This passage has paragraphs, but there are no chapters. Choices A, B, and C are incorrect. This passage is a story with a beginning, middle, and end. The correct answer is choice D.

At the beginning of the story, the author introduces the main characters. Who are the main characters in the story?

A Baker and Farmer

B Cat and Mouse

C Cow and Cat

D Mouse and Farmer

The story begins with Cat and Mouse playing. Cat and Mouse are the main characters in the story. Mouse is trying to get his tail back from Cat. The correct answer is choice B.

At the very beginning, where does the story take place?

    A in the cellar

    B in a field

    C in the kitchen

    D in a barn

The story begins with Cat and Mouse playing in the barn. This is the **setting** of the story. The story does not begin in a cellar, field, or kitchen. Choices A, B, and C are incorrect. Choice D is the correct answer.

What is the problem at the beginning of the story?

    A Cow wants hay.

    B Farmer wants bread.

    C Mouse wants his tail.

    D Cat wants milk.

The problem at the beginning of the story is that Cat bit off Mouse's tail. The problem is also called the **conflict** of a story. Mouse wants Cat to give his tail back. But Cat wants some milk first. The correct answer is choice C. Mouse wants his tail back.

UNIT 3 ▓▓
Craft and Structure

In the middle of the story, how does Mouse try to solve his problem?

_____

_____

_____

_____

✓ **Think about what Cat tells Mouse to do and what happens in the story. Here is a sample answer:**

Mouse goes to other characters. He has to keep trading favors. Mouse asks Cow for milk, but Cow wants hay from Farmer. Mouse runs to Farmer. He asks Farmer for hay, but Farmer wants bread from Baker. Mouse runs to Baker. Everyone wants something more from Mouse.

What happens at the end of the story to solve the problem?

_____

_____

✓ **Does Mouse get his tail back? Here is a sample answer:**

At the end of the story, Mouse gets milk for Cat. Then Cat gives back Mouse's tail.

How does the author make you want to read on?

_____

_____

_____

 Authors like to create suspense. This means that the reader waits to find out what will happen. Here is a sample answer:

> Every time Mouse asks for something, he must get something else. This makes the reader wonder who Mouse will need to go to next. What will Mouse need to get? How many times will this happen? Will Mouse ever get his tail back?

How does the author use repetition in this story?

_____

_____

_____

 Mouse keeps doing something in the story. What is it? Here is a sample answer:

> First, Mouse runs from Cat to Cow. Then he runs from Cow to Farmer. Last, he runs from Farmer to Baker. Then he must repeat the same steps, only backwards. The author builds the story by repeating these steps. The author uses the same words again and again.

If you could add one more person for Mouse to visit in this story, who would you add?

_____

_____

_____

 This question asks you to use your imagination and what you know about the story. There are many good ideas to make the story longer. Here is a sample answer:

One idea is to add a Butcher to the story. Baker asks Mouse to get him some meat from Butcher. Then Baker will give Mouse some bread.

Test Yourself

Little Robin Redbreast

1   Little Robin Redbreast
2   Sat up in a tree,
3   Up climbed sneaky Kitty Cat,
4   "It is lunchtime!" thought he.
5   Robin Redbreast saw him come,
6   And quickly flew away,
7   Said Little Robin Redbreast,
8   "You won't eat me today;
9   No, you won't eat me today!"

10 Little Robin Redbreast
11 Flew up to a wall,
12 Kitty tried to follow
13 But the wall was too tall!
14 Little Robin Redbreast laughed and chirped,
15 And what did Kitty say?
16 "Meow, meow, I guess there won't be
17 Any lunch for me today;
18 No lunch for me today!"

1 How many stanzas are in this poem?

   A one

   B two

   C nine

   D eighteen

2 Where is Robin Redbreast at the beginning of this poem?

    A in a tree

    B on a wall

    C in the garden

    D at the window

3 Who are the characters in this poem?

    A a boy and a robin

    B a boy and a cat

    C a robin and a cat

    D a mouse and a robin

4 Explain what the problem is at the start of the poem.

_____

_____

_____

_____

5 Read lines 3 and 4 of the poem.

   Up climbed sneaky Kitty Cat,
   "It is lunchtime!" thought he.

What do these words make you think might happen next?

   A Kitty Cat will fall off the wall.

   B Kitty Cat will go home to eat.

   C Kitty Cat will make friends.

   D Kitty Cat will catch the robin.

6 What happens to the Little Robin Redbreast and Kitty Cat at the end of the poem?

_____

_____

_____

_____

7 Choose the words that rhyme in the second stanza of the poem.

   A tree and today

   B meow, meow

   C wall and tall

   D cat and come

UNIT 3 ✖✖✖✖✖✖✖✖✖✖✖✖✖✖✖✖✖✖✖✖✖✖✖✖✖✖✖✖✖✖✖✖✖✖
Craft and Structure

8 Clap the rhythm as you read lines 5 and 6 of the poem.

> *Robin Redbreast saw him come,*
> *And quickly flew away.*

How many beats do you hear?

A four

B five

C six

D seven

9 Which does the poet use in the names Robin Redbreast and Kitty Cat?

A repeated words

B rhyming words

C repeated beginning sounds

D actual sounds a person would hear

10 Why does the poet *most* likely use repeated words at the end of the poem?

_____

_____

_____

_____

Text Features

RI.2.5

Nonfiction writing has special text features. There are headings on the pages. There are words in bold print. There are pictures with captions. There is a table of contents in the front of the book. There is a glossary and an index in the back. Web pages have menus and icons. These tools help readers learn more. They make text easier to read.

Text Features

Writers use larger, darker print for **headings.** This dark print is called **bold** print. Headings break text into smaller chunks. They make text easier to read. Look at the headings in the passage on the next page. The first heading tells what this chunk is about. It is about bears. The second heading is called a **subheading.** The subheading tells that the next chunk is about one type of bear. This is the polar bear. The next subheading tells that this text is about another type of bear. This is about the grizzly bear.

The photographs give more information about the subject. They show what the bears look like. The sentence under a photograph is a **caption.** This sentence tells more about the photograph. Captions can be very helpful.

Different Types of Bears

Bears are very large and heavy animals. They have thick, shaggy fur and short tails. Their small round ears stick straight up. Bears have short, powerful legs and large feet. They may look slow, but bears can move very quickly. Bears use their claws to dig and tear to find food. They eat plants, honey, insects, fish, and small animals. Bears live alone. They spend much of the winter sleeping. There are many kinds of bears, such as a brown bear, black bear, polar bear, and grizzly bear.

Polar Bears

Polar bears are the largest bears in the world. They are big, strong, and heavy. Polar bears live near the North Pole, near the Arctic Ocean. They are built to survive in the harsh, frozen north. Their white fur helps them sneak up on prey on the ice and snow. Their padded paws and sharp claws help them walk on ice and snow.

Polar bears are meat-eaters. They hunt seals, walruses, and even whales. A polar bear is very patient. It will sit by a hole in the ice for hours and wait for a seal to come up for air. A polar bear can kill a seal with just one swipe of its strong paw.

After eating, polar bears wash themselves with water or snow.

Polar bears are very good swimmers. Their long body shape helps them move through the water. Their ears are small and close to the head. Their noses, heads, and necks are long. Polar bear have padded paws with short claws. Webbed paws and short, strong legs make them fast swimmers.

Grizzly Bears

Like polar bears, grizzly bears are very large and strong. They eat almost anything. They will eat grass, roots, berries, insects, fish, and even moose. They are mostly found in North America and Canada. You probably will not find one near your home. They live in mountains and forests far away from humans.

Grizzly bears go to sleep for the winter, or hibernate. They do this for 5–8 months. When they are not sleeping, they are finding food. They have to store enough fat on their body for winter.

Grizzly bear and her cubs looking for food in a river.

Glossary and Index

A **glossary** and an **index** are tools to help the reader. They are found in the back of books. A glossary lists words in ABC order. It tells their meanings, like a dictionary. Next time you read a book, note the bold print words. These are **key words.** You will find them in the glossary.

An index lists subjects in ABC order. It shows page numbers. Readers turn to these pages in the book to learn about a subject. See the sample glossary and index on the right.

Glossary

beagle	A small hound dog with short legs and drooping ears
bear	Large, heavy mammals with shaggy fur and a short tail
beaver	A large rodent with soft brown fur and a flat broad tail

Index

beagle, 2–3, 9, 13
bear, 27–29, 42, 56
beaver, 16–17, 19

Menus and Icons

Writers use text features on web pages, too. **Menus** and **icons** help readers find more information. Readers click on an icon. The screen shows the reader more about the topic. Readers can click on a menu to open a list. The list drops down. It gives the reader more choices. It helps readers find what they need.

Click on the polar bear icon. A menu opens. The menu lists things about polar bears. To find out about where polar bears live, click on habitat. More about where polar bears live shows on the screen.

Guided Practice

Read the two passages. Then answer the questions.

Passage 1

Choosing the Right Pet

Fluffy puppies and furry kittens are so cute. It is fun to pet them and play with them. They are warm and cuddly to hold. You want to rush home with a new little bundle of fur. But before you decide to get a new pet, take time to think.

Cats are so easy to love.

What Do Pets Do for Us?

Pets bring us great joy. They become part of our family. There are many different kinds of pets. There are pets that fit with where we live and pets that do not. There are pets that need more time and energy than others do. There are pets that fit our lifestyles and pets that do not. There are pets that have special needs. There are lots of pets that need good homes. It is important to think carefully about which pet is right for you and your family.

What Do Pets Need from Us?

Having a pet takes time. Pets need attention, love, and respect. They need food, water, toys, and supplies. They need to be kept safe. Some pets can not be left alone. Other pets need lots of space. They need exercise and training. Pets need trips to the vet, shots, and medicine. Some pets need grooming. Most pets live a long time. They will need a good home for many, many years.

Questions to Ask Yourself

What kind of pet is best for me and my family?

Does everyone in my family want a pet?

What kind of pet is best for my home?

How much time do I have to spend with a pet?

How much space do I have for my pet inside my home?

Do I have a safe outdoor place to exercise a pet?

Puppies need playtime every day.

Can I afford to feed a pet?

Can I afford to take care of a pet if it gets injured or sick?

Is there anyone to help me care for a pet?

Is anyone in my home allergic to animals?

Having a pet is an important decision. Take time to think it through. Then find the pet that is just right for you.

Passage 2

http://www.petsafety.com

| Welcome | Indoor Dangers | Plants | Humans | Other Pets | Outdoor Dangers |

Keep Your Pet Safe

Share Your Pet Danger Story
Send us your story.
Help others learn to protect their pets.
⬥ Click to Submit

Because we love our pets, we want to keep them safe. Nothing takes the place of watching your pet at all times. But that is not always possible.

Pets are in more danger at home than outdoors. Garbage, people, food, and medicine can poison pets. Decorations can cause choking. Electric cords and toys can harm pets.

Some plants are poisonous if eaten. Find out if a plant is toxic before you bring it indoors. Keep these plants out of reach. Keep your pet away from toxic outdoor plants.

Accidents happen. Be careful not to step on, kick, or hurt your pet in any way.

Having other people around can cause pets harm. We get busy with our guests. We ignore the needs of our pets. Pets need extra attention. Let your guests know the pet rules in your house. Tell them where your pet is allowed to go. Tell them what your pet can eat. Never let anyone tease your pet.

Glossary

decorations	Items put up around the house for holidays
medicine	Anything used to treat an injury or illness
poison	Something that can cause illness or death when eaten
toxic	Affected by or caused by something that is poisonous

Pets that do not get along with each other can cause harm. Introduce a new pet to the other pets in your home. Be sure that they can get along before bringing home a new pet.

http://www.petsafety.com

There are many pet dangers outdoors. Very hot or very cold weather can be deadly. Insects, bad water, and wild animals can harm your pet. Cars and trucks can harm or kill pets. Always keep your pet under safe control outdoors.

Click on the icons at the top of the web page to learn more about pet dangers.

Passage 1 is organized as a _____.

   A magazine article

   B web page

   C glossary

   D index

Passage 1 is not a web page. There are no icons or menus. It is not a glossary or an index. It is a magazine article. The text of the article has headings. There are pictures with captions. Choice A is the correct answer.

How is passage 2 organized?

   A   as a magazine article

   B   as a textbook page

   C   as a web page

   D   as a poem

The second passage is not a magazine article or a textbook page. There are no headings or pictures with captions. It is not a poem. There are no lines and stanzas. There is no rhythm or rhyme. Choices A, B, and D are incorrect. It is organized as a web page. There are icons to click on to find more information. The correct answer is choice C.

In passage 2, what text feature could help you find the meaning of the word <u>toxic</u>?

_____

_____

_____

_____

Think about what text features explain what a word means. Here is a sample answer:

   To find the meaning of the word <u>toxic</u>, look in the glossary. This text feature is a tool. It helps readers find words and their meanings. Then readers can understand what they read.

Where would you look in passage 2 to find out more about dangers from other pets?

_____

_____

> ✓ **Look at the text features in passage 2. Do any of them lead to more information? Here is a sample answer:**

You would click on an icon. The Other Pets icon is the best bet. It will tell more about pet dangers from other pets.

How do headings in passage 1 make the text easier to understand?

_____

_____

_____

> ✓ **Headings make the text easier to understand. Think about the page if there were no headings. Why would it be harder to read? Here is a sample answer:**

Headings break down text. They show us where to read to find information. Each part of the text builds on the part before it. Breaking down text makes it easier to read and understand.

Test Yourself

Passage 1

| Home | 🐕 Puppy Training | 🐕 Obedience Training | Leash Training | Crate Training |

Doggone Good Dog Training

A good dog is more fun. Give your dog the best training. Doggone Good Dog Training can make you and your dog feel relaxed around family and friends.

Doggone Good Dog Training lessons are short and fun. Step-by-step training uses praise and rewards. Learn to communicate with your dog. Learn to set boundaries and stick to them. Build a strong bond with your best friend. No more barking, chewing, digging, or jumping up! All you need is patience and love.

You can have a happier and safer dog with Doggone Good Dog Training. Click on the icons above for more information.

New classes are starting soon.

 Register now for Doggone Good Dog Training!

How to Start a Pet-Sitting Business

Most people are spending much less money these days. But people are still spending money on their pets. And you could make money, too.

Why People Need Pet Sitters

Some pet owners work long hours. They do not like to leave their pets alone. Bored pets get into trouble. Pets need play and exercise. It makes pet owners feel better to have someone check on their pet. People like to leave their pets in their own homes. Sending a pet to a kennel is upsetting for pets and their owners.

How to Get Started

If you like animals, think about starting a pet-sitting business. **Start slowly. It takes time to build a business.** Get the word out. Talk to family members, neighbors, and friends. Put up signs at the local vet and pet stores. Create a pet-sitting website.

Begin as a dog walker and build up your business.

How to Get Ready

Go online or go to the library. Study dog and cat care. You may want to take a pet First Aid course. Join a pet-sitting organization that gives classes. You can meet and talk to other pet sitters.

Begin with small steps. You may want to start as a dog walker. Then work up to feeding pets. Build your business.

How to Be Successful

Set your business apart. Offer special rates for senior citizens or people with more than one pet. Give out coupons at first time visits. Offer a free visit before your first pet-sitting job.

1 What text feature in passage 1 helps you register for Doggone Good Dog Training classes?

A icon

B menu

C glossary

D photograph

2 A customer wants to read more about training a dog to obey commands. Which icon in passage 1 would help?

A leash training

B obedience training

C crate training

D puppy training

3 Which *best* describes the text features in passage 1?

A glossary and index

B headings

C captions

D icon and menus

4 Which of these *best* describes how the information in passage 2 is organized?

A textbook page

B web page

C diary entry

D magazine article

5 What text feature in passage 2 breaks down the information about starting a pet-sitting business?

A captions

B headings

C bold print

D glossary

6 In passage 2, what does the author want you to understand about the picture?

A dogs need plenty of exercise

B start your business as a dog walker

C always walk dogs on a leash

D walk dogs for at least 10 minutes

7 Why did the authors organize the information in the two passages in the ways that they did?

_____

_____

_____

_____

_____

8 If you could write a glossary for passage 1, which words would you list? Explain why a glossary would be a useful tool.

_____

_____

_____

_____

_____

Point of View and Author's Purpose

RL.2.6, RI.2.6

Authors write for their own reasons. The **author's purpose** is the reason why an author writes something. All writing has a **point of view.** Nonfiction writing has a point of view. Would you enjoy reading a story about rats? The author may have a pet rat. The author thinks rats are cute and fun. That is his point of view. A lady who found a rat in her kitchen would have a very different point of view. Each story is told in a different way. Each story feels different to the reader.

A story or poem has a point of view, too. It can be told from the point of view of one or more characters. It can be told from the point of view of someone outside the story.

It is important to think about *who* is telling a story. *Why* is the author writing? *Who* is the author? *How* does the author want me to feel? Always ask *who, how* and *why* when you read.

The Author's Purpose in Informational Text

The author's purpose is the reason for writing. It is *why* the author writes something. Informational text is all about facts and ideas. Authors write these texts for four reasons:

- to explain, or to teach something
- to persuade, or to get the reader to do or believe something
- to describe, or to tell about something
- to entertain, or for fun or pleasure.

The Circus is Coming to Town!

Come to the Funniest Show in America!
The Clown Car Circus is coming to your town!

Silly clowns! Magic tricks! Funny jokes!
Balloon animals! Tumbling! Amazing animals!

Clowns with dogs! Clowns in cars!
Clowns playing music! Juggling clowns!

Funny faces, baggy pants, and big shoes!
The Clown Car Circus has them all!

Clown Car Circus clowns are the best clowns
in the world!

June 3–10

Downtown Park

Big top opens at 7 p.m.

Kids can win a prize!
Wear a clown costume on Kids Clown Night, June 5.

What is the author's purpose in this passage?

    A to get readers to come to the circus

    B to tell readers that clowns are scary

    C to tell readers that they can be clowns

    D to get readers to buy clown costumes

The author is trying to get people to come to a circus here. He is trying to persuade. Choice A is the correct answer. The author does not tell about scary clowns. He does not describe how to be a clown. And he does not tell how to buy clown costumes. Choices B, C, and D are incorrect.

Who do you think this was written for?

    A people who do not like circuses

    B people who like clowns

    C children

    D everyone

This passage is an advertisement. It is written to persuade many people to come to the circus. Choice D is the correct answer.

The Greatest Show on Earth

The circus began in America 200 years ago. It was started by a young man. His name was P. T. Barnum. He liked to make people laugh. He liked to make money, too. Barnum found interesting people for his circus. He found a lady with a long beard. He found little people. He found the tallest man in the world. Barnum found strange animals. Barnum found a cow with two heads. He found a jumbo elephant. He put them in his circus.

Barnum put up big posters. People came to see his circus. The shows were inside a big tent. People saw jugglers. They saw clowns. They watched people juggling and spinning plates. People were amazed! The circus grew and grew. The Greatest Show on Earth traveled across America by train. It was one mile long!

What is the main purpose of this passage?

A to get children to come to the show

B to describe how P. T. Barnum liked to laugh

C to explain how P. T. Barnum started the Greatest Show on Earth

D to tell readers that P.T. Barnum only cared about making money

This passage explains. It tells how and why P. T. Barnum started the Greatest Show on Earth. It does not try to persuade or describe anything more than this. Choice C is the correct answer.

Where would you *most* likely find a passage like this?

A in a magazine

B on a poster

C in a letter to the editor

D on a page of directions

This passage is too long for a poster. Posters are meant to advertise something. This passage tells about something. It does not give a strong enough view for a letter to the editor. It is not directions. The correct answer is choice A.

What is the author's point of view of P. T. Barnum?

A He was strange.

B He was funny.

C He was greedy.

D He was successful.

The author paints a picture of P. T. Barnum in words. He does not say he was strange or greedy. There is nothing to show he was funny. Choices A, B, and C are incorrect. The author does suggest P. T. Barnum was successful. Choice D is the correct answer.

shabby
not well kept

Learn How to Be a Clown

Do you like to make people laugh? You can learn to be a clown.

Just follow these easy steps:

1. Choose the kind of clown that is most like you. Choose a clown that likes to do what you like to do. Are you a girl or a boy clown? Are you a fancy clown or a shabby clown? Are you a goofy clown or a scared clown? Are you a prankster clown or a serious clown? Are you a baby clown or an old clown? Are you a dancing clown or a clumsy clown?

2. Choose a name that fits your clown. Your name can fit how you look, how you act, or what you do. You can add other words to your real name.

3. Choose a costume for your clown. Find clothes in thrift shops that fit your kind of clown. Use clothes that are too small or too big. Use clothes that do not match. Use hats, glasses, suspenders, or other items for your costume. Look for clown noses, ears, and shoes in costume stores.

4. Choose your clown face. First, draw and color your clown face on paper. Use make-up to cover your face. Then use bright colors to show off your eyes, nose, cheeks or mouth.

5. Choose your act. Think about what you do that makes people laugh. Can you speak in a funny voice? Can you play music? Can you tumble? How can you do something in a silly way? What props do you need?

What is the author's purpose for writing this passage?

    A to entertain with a story about clowns

    B to persuade children to be clowns

    C to tell about clown college

    D to explain the steps in how to be a clown

This passage does not tell a story. It does not try to get the reader to do anything. And it does not explain what clown college is. Choices A, B, and C are incorrect. It does explain the steps in becoming a clown. The best answer is choice D.

Who is *most* likely the author of this passage?

    A someone who wants to be a clown

    B someone who teaches clown school

    C someone who is afraid of clowns

    D someone who knows a clown

We have to think about who would write directions. Who would know this information? It would probably be a teacher of clowns. Choice B is the correct answer.

Point of View in Literary Text

Stories have points of view, too. When you read, you must ask yourself, *Who is telling the story?*

The person telling a story is the **narrator.** Some stories are told from one character's point of view. This is called **first-person point of view.** You can tell because the person telling the story uses the word *I* or *you.* Stories can also be told from the point of view of another character in the story. It can be told by more than one character. Or, it can be told by someone who is outside the story. This is called **third-person point of view.** You can tell because these stories use *he, she,* and *they.*

Poems have a point of view, too. The person telling a poem is the **speaker.** The speaker may be a character. Or, the speaker may tell the point of view of someone outside the poem.

Guided Practice

Read the poem. Then answer the questions.

My Side of the Story

Old Mother Goose wrote down this poem. Most children think it is true.

1 Little Miss Muffet,
2 Sat on a tuffet[1],
3 Eating her curds and whey[2];
4 Along came a spider,
5 Who sat down beside her,
6 And frightened Miss Muffet away.

---

[1]**tuffet:** stool

[2] **curds and whey:** cheese like cottage cheese

But no one ever heard *my* side. Please, let me share it with you.

1 This little old spider
2 Would never hurt her;
3 Just doing what all spiders do,
4 I was spinning away
5 On my web that fine day,
6 To catch me a fat fly or two.

7 When Little Miss Muffet,
8 Plopped down on the tuffet,
9 To lunch on some fine cottage cheese.
10 I was not excited,
11 She was not invited,
12 She never asked, "May I?" or "Please?"

13 Now the part that I dread—
14 When the hat on her head,
15 Caused my new web to go flying;
16 Straight down I dropped,
17 Beside her I plopped,
18 Missy Muffet ran away crying.

19 It was not the wee spider,
20 That sat down beside her,
21 Who caused all the trouble, I say.
22 It was Little Miss Muffet,
23 The girl on the tuffet,
24 Who forgot her manners that day.

From whose point of view is the nursery rhyme "Little Miss Muffet" written?

A Miss Muffet

B a speaker

C the spider

D the tuffet

Miss Muffet does not tell the story. The spider does not tell the story either. A tuffet cannot tell a story. The story is told by a speaker outside the story. The speaker looks in and tells what is happening. The correct answer is choice B.

Who is the speaker in the new poem "My Side of the Story"?

A Miss Muffet

B the spider

C an outside speaker

D Miss Muffet's mother

The speaker in the new poem is not Miss Muffet or her mother. It is not a speaker outside the story. Choices A, C, and D are incorrect. The poem is told from the point of view of the spider. The spider is telling his side of the story of the old rhyme. Choice B is the correct answer.

Which choice *best* describes the point of view in the new poem "My Side of the Story"?

A Do not mess with spiders or they will eat your lunch!

B Everyone knows that Miss Muffet is a polite little girl.

C It is not fair to blame the spider for scaring Miss Muffet.

D The spider had fun scaring Little Miss Muffet away.

The new poem is written from the spider's point of view. The spider says he did nothing wrong. It is not fair to blame him for scaring Miss Muffet away. Choice C is the correct answer.

Which choice *best* describes the author's purpose in the new poem?

A to explain

B to describe

C to persuade

D to entertain

The poem "My Side of the Story" does not explain. It does not describe. The author does not try to entertain the reader. The correct answer is choice C. The author writes to persuade us that the spider did nothing wrong.

Test Yourself

Passage 1

Lemonade for Sale

Take time to cool off. Meet your neighbors.
Talk to your friends.

Enjoy a cup of ice-cold lemonade!

Lemonade stands are popping up all over town. Students from our schools are hard at work. This weekend, they will be selling homemade lemonade. They want to make one thousand dollars. They want to build a display for children at the park.

Bring the grandparents. Bring the aunts and uncles. Bring the cousins. Bring the dog. Come down to River Town this Saturday and Sunday. Buy lemonade for just 75¢ a cup. Stands will be open from 10 a.m. until 5 p.m.

Come and have some fun. Check out the bright, colorful lemonade stands. See our kids in action. Taste the lemonade. Vote for your favorite. Which lemonade will become River Town's Official Favorite this year?

Help our kids. Help our town.

Lemonade Days

It happens every year. It happens for three days in June. People sell lemonade all across America. They make money to fight cancer. They call it Lemonade Days.

It started with a four-year-old girl. She was in the hospital. The little girl had cancer. She wanted to get better. She wanted to have a lemonade stand. The little girl wanted to help the doctors at her hospital. She wanted them to find a cure for cancer.

Soon she felt better. The little girl went home. She opened a lemonade stand. She and her brother worked hard to raise money. It took them four years. But they made more than one million dollars.

The little girl's family kept raising money. They started Alex's Lemonade Stand Foundation. The foundation made more than ten million dollars. They gave it to the doctors and scientists. The doctors and scientists work to find cures for children's cancer.

Falling for Skiing

I remember the moment well. I was swish-swashing over little mounds of snow, making my way down the hill on my super-cool skis. I waved to my buddy, Len, and whoops. I fell down, down, down the hill. When I got to the bottom, I could not move my leg. The snow ski team came out and put me on a stretcher. Yep, it was broken alright. So now I sit in my room every day just dreaming about getting back on my skis before the winter snow melts.

"Taylor," my mom yells.

"Yes," I say back, as I am limited to my bedroom for now.

"We got you a surprise," my mother says as she enters my room.

"What is it?" I say as I dream she is bringing me new skis.

"It's a book about skiing!" says my mom.

"For what?" I ask.

"The doctor says you will be stuck in your bed for days. We want you to be able to have some entertainment," my mom says.

"Oh," I say, as I am not that into books.

"Look," she points out. "You can research your favorite skiers. You can study their moves. Then maybe you won't fall again."

I smile as large as I can. "I have the greatest mom ever."

"Thanks!" she says as she gives me a hug.

1 What is the author's purpose in writing passage 1?

    A to describe or explain something

    B to persuade someone to do something

    C to tell someone how to do something

    D to tell a funny story about lemonade

2 From whose point of view is passage 1 written?

    A someone who has a dog

    B someone who likes lemonade

    C someone who wants to go to River Town

    D someone who wants people to give money

3 Why did the author write passage 2?

    A to make the reader feel sad

    B to make people afraid of cancer

    C to show what people can do help cure cancer

    D to help the reader build a lemonade stand

4 From whose point of view is passage 3 written?

   A Taylor

   B Taylor's mom

   C an outside narrator

   D an outside speaker

5 Which *best* tells the author's purpose in passage 3?

   A to entertain

   B to describe

   C to persuade

   D to explain

REVIEW

Craft and Structure

Vocabulary
dreary
pardon
spare
trill

Read the poem. Then answer the questions.

Five Fluffy Little Robins

1 Five fluffy little robins,
2 Looked up at the sky.
3 It was time to leave the nest,
4 And find out how to fly.

5 Four flitter-fluttered off,
6 But one was full of fear.
7 He said, "It's far too high,
8 I think I'll stay right here!"

9 "Come on!" said the others,
10 Flying freely in the sun.
11 So their little brother tried it
12 And found that it was fun.

1 Which of these *best* describes the structure of this poem?

   A three paragraphs

   B three chapters

   C three scenes

   D three stanzas

2 What is the point of view of this poem?

   A the speaker is someone who speaks for the nest

   B the speaker is someone outside the passage who tells what happens

   C the speaker is someone who speaks for one of the robins

   D the speaker is someone who speaks for all five robins

3 Which lines rhyme in each stanza of this poem?

   A lines 1 and 2

   B lines 2 and 3

   C lines 1 and 3

   D lines 2 and 4

4 What happens at the end of this poem?

   A All five robins return to the nest.

   B The last robin leaves the nest.

   C Four robins leave the nest, but one stays behind.

   D One robin leaves the nest, but four stay behind.

UNIT 3 ✖✖
Craft and Structure

5 What is special about line 5?

    A Words are repeated.

    B Sounds are repeated.

    C There are rhyming words.

    D There is a 10-beat rhythm.

Read the poem. Then answer the questions.

The Chickadee-dee

1   Little darling of the snow,
2   Careless how the winds may blow,
3   Happy as a bird can be,
4   Singing, oh, so cheerily,
5   Chickadee-dee! Chickadee-dee!

6   When the skies are cold and gray,
7   When he trills[1] his happiest lay,
8   Through the clouds he seems to see
9   Hidden things to you and me.
10   Chickadee-dee! Chickadee-dee!

11   Very likely little birds
12   Have their thoughts too deep for words,
13   But we know, and all agree,
14   That the world would dreary[2] be
15   Without birds, dear chickadee!

---

trill: vibrating sound like the warbling song of a bird

dreary: sad and dull

6 What word does the author use to make the sound of a chickadee?

A dreary

B singing

C happiest

D chickadee-dee!

7 How does the speaker describe chickadees?

A hidden and deep

B happy and cheerful

C sad and dreary

D careless and afraid

Pardon Me, Mr. President

The Old Way

It was the old way. In November, people met at the White House. They gave a live turkey to President Truman. He looked it over. He gave the turkey a name. He smiled for pictures with it. The President of the United States wished America a happy Thanksgiving. He would see that turkey again. The turkey would be cooked for his Thanksgiving dinner! It was the same year after year.

President Obama officially pardons a Thanksgiving turkey named "Courage."

The Last Twenty Years

President John F. Kennedy felt bad for the turkey. He did not want to eat it. He said he wanted to keep the bird. Maybe he did. The first president to spare the turkey's life was George H. W. Bush. President Bill Clinton saved eight turkeys. Then, President George W. Bush saved eight of them. Last year, President Obama pardoned his first White House turkey.

Presidents Who Received Thanksgiving Turkeys

Harry S. Truman	1945–1953
Dwight D. Eisenhower	1953–1961
John F. Kennedy	1961–1963
Lyndon B. Johnson	1963–1969
Richard Nixon	1969–1974
Gerald Ford	1974–1977
Jimmy Carter	1977–1981
Ronald Reagan	1981–1989
George H. W. Bush	1989–1993
Bill Clinton	1993–2001
George W. Bush	2001–2009
Barack Obama	2009–present

A New Way

Now there is a new way. The president gets a turkey. He names the turkey. He pardons the turkey. The turkey is saved from the White House dinner table. The turkey goes to Disneyland. It leads the Thanksgiving Day parade. The bird spends the rest of its life there. Lucky turkey!

Glossary

pardon   to let go or excuse
spare   to save

8 The text feature "The Last Twenty Years" is _____.

   A an icon

   B a caption

   C a key word

   D a heading

9 Which text feature tells the meaning of the word pardon?

   A sidebar

   B caption

   C heading

   D glossary

10 What is the author's purpose in writing the passage?

   A to entertain

   B to persuade

   C to describe

   D to explain

UNIT 3 ▨▨▨▨▨▨▨▨▨▨▨▨▨▨▨▨▨▨▨▨▨▨▨▨▨▨▨▨▨▨▨▨▨▨
Craft and Structure

Integration of Knowledge and Ideas

UNIT 4

When you read stories, you can compare things. First, read one text. Then read another. What is the same about them? What is different? Doing this helps you understand what you read.

When you look at text and pictures, you can see new things. You can fill in the blanks in your stories. Ask yourself what you learn from the pictures that might not be in the words.

This unit is all about how you get information from what you read. It is about using the information you get from the text. It is about doing things with that information.

- **In Lesson 11,** you will learn how visual elements can help you learn about what you read.

- **Lesson 12** is about what you read in your texts. You will learn about facts and opinions. You will learn that some things do not have proof, and some do.

- **In Lesson 13,** you will learn to look at texts to see what is the same about them. You will look for things that are different. These things will help you get the most out of what you read.

Visual Literacy

RL.2.7, RI.2.7

Vocabulary
allergic
crust
rotate

Think about your favorite book. Does it have pictures? When you are in school, are there pictures in the books you use? Pictures, charts, and maps can help us learn. They add meaning and information to the words that we read.

Guided Practice

Read the passage. Then answer the questions.

The Garden

allergic
getting sick when around animal hair, plants, or foods that do not bother other people

I have always wanted a pet, like a cat or a dog, but I am allergic. My allergies make it so I cannot have pets. I was really upset about this for a long time. My mom and dad tried to make me feel better, but I really wanted something to take care of. I wanted to love something and help it grow! A lot of my friends have pets. I am one of the only people in second grade at my school who does not have one.

So the other day, my mom and dad gave me a surprise! They brought me outside. We walked around to our back yard. There was a patch of dirt in one corner. "What is this dirt?" I said.

"This will be your garden!" they said. They told me that I could grow something in it, and that it would be sort of like a pet. I would have to take care of whatever I grew!

So now I grow plants, and I water them every day. I may not have a pet, but at least I have something to take care of!

Which detail of the story is *best* shown by the pictures?

A The main character is allergic to animals.

B The main character was surprised by the garden.

C The main character's parents gave him a gift of a garden.

D The main character is the only student who does not have a pet.

Look at the pictures. They show a garden. This is a clue that you should look at choices B or C. They both have the word <u>garden</u> in them. But we do not see the main character being surprised in either of these pictures. We do see the gift of the garden. The correct answer is choice C.

How do the pictures add to what you know about the story?

_____

_____

_____

✓ **Look at what is happening in each picture. Here is a sample answer:**

The story does not tell us that his parents helped him. The first picture shows that his parents taught him how to plant his garden.

Do you think that the narrator grew vegetables or flowers?

_____

_____

✓ **The pictures give you details that the story does not. Here is a sample answer:**

He grew flowers. One picture shows him planting flower bulbs. Another shows flowers. Neither shows vegetables.

UNIT 4 ▪▪▪▪▪▪▪▪▪▪▪▪▪▪▪▪▪▪▪▪▪▪▪▪▪▪▪▪▪▪▪▪▪▪▪▪▪
Integration of Knowledge and Ideas

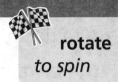

rotate
to spin

How Lawn Mowers Work

Many people do not like to mow the lawn. But, the machines we use to do it are interesting. Have you ever wondered how they work?

The first lawn mowers did not have engines. As time went on, they got more advanced. Today, lawn mowers have blades that rotate. They spin fast enough to cut the grass as they touch it.

The blade is in something called a "deck." The deck keeps the grass from flying all over the place when you mow it. Imagine what a mess it would be without the deck!

The deck is on top of wheels. The motor that powers the mower sits on top of the deck. Some mowers also have bags attached. The bag catches the grass clippings.

Usually, you push these mowers. There are also mowers you can ride on, though! These mowers make sense for people with very large yards.

Whatever kind of mower you use, the way the blades work is pretty similar. They have come a long way from the push mowers with no motor!

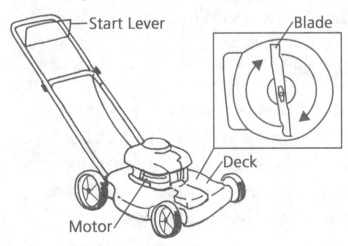

Start Lever

Blade

Deck

Motor

Which of these is *best* shown by the picture?

A a riding mower

B how a mower's blades move

C a mower with no engine

D a mower with a bag attached to it

> The picture shows the lawn mower and its blades. It also shows you arrows that give you an idea of the way the blades move, or rotate. This helps you understand the text. Choice B is the correct answer.

Name one detail that the picture helps you understand about how mowers work.

_____

_____

_____

_____

_____

> Think about what the text tells you. Then look closely at the picture. Here is a sample answer:

You can see the parts of the lawn mower. The text says that some mowers have bags, but the one in the picture does not. The picture shows the start lever. The text does not explain how to start the mower. The picture also shows that the mower has more wheels than a push mower.

Name one detail from the text that is not shown in the picture.

_____

_____

Again, you have to pay close attention to the text and to the illustration. Here is a sample answer:

There are a few things not shown. One is the bag. The mower in the picture does not have a bag on it.

Imagine that your teacher asked you to write a report about lawn mowers. Using the text AND the picture, list four things you could include in it.

_____

_____

_____

Think about what you learned about mowers. What did you learn from the text? What did you learn from the picture? Here is a sample answer:

The report could include many things. One is that the blades are covered by the deck. Some mowers are riding mowers, and some are push mowers. You could also say some mowers have a bag on them. The blades rotate very fast to cut the grass.

Passage 1

The Spelling Bee

The big spelling bee was right around the corner, and I was ready! I had stayed up late for a few days, studying my heart out, and I could spell any word that came my way!

The spelling bee was a big deal at my school. Everyone stood on a big stage, and all the parents watched. There was a big crowd! And I felt that I could really win!

The big day finally arrived. My class lined up, single file, on stage. I looked out into the crowd—uh oh! The crowd was so big! I had not expected all those people; how would I ever go up in front of them?

I had stage fright, no doubt about it! I was too nervous to even walk up to the microphone!

Finally, my name was called. "Jenny?" the voice said. "Jenny, please come up to spell your word." My knees shook, my hands were sweaty, and my face turned red.

I walked slowly to the microphone. The teacher gave me my word. I closed my eyes tight, and… I spelled it right! I did it!

But, my stage fright taught me something: I should not have been so overconfident! I did not win the spelling bee that day, but I did a great job anyway! It was not all about winning; it was about trying something new!

Passage 2

How Microwaves Work

Pop! Pop! Do you smell popcorn? Chances are you have smelled popcorn made in a microwave oven before. How does the microwave make the popcorn? How does it make other food?

Microwave ovens use—you guessed it—microwaves to heat food. <u>Micro</u> means "small." The waves are a kind of radio wave. These waves are absorbed by fat and sugars. When they are absorbed, the waves turn into heat. This is how they cook the food.

The heat in a microwave is different from an oven. The oven's air heats up and forms a crust on the food it cooks. A microwave's air is not that hot. So the food does not form a crust.

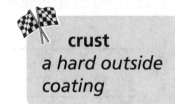

crust
a hard outside coating

The heat enters the food fast and the food heats evenly. It does not overcook the outside quickly.

The waves that cook the food are not absorbed by metal. Metal should not be used in a microwave. You should use glass.

Microwaves have changed the way we can make our food.

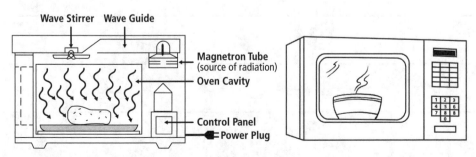

Wave Stirrer   Wave Guide
Magnetron Tube (source of radiation)
Oven Cavity
Control Panel
Power Plug

1 In passage 1, which of these details is *best* shown by the picture?

   A Jenny was ready for the spelling bee.

   B Jenny had never been in a spelling bee before.

   C When Jenny went to spell her word, she got very nervous.

   D If Jenny won this spelling bee, she would go on to more spelling bees.

2 What does the picture with passage 1 show you? How does it relate to the story?

_____

_____

_____

_____

3 What is the purpose of the picture shown with passage 2?

_____

_____

_____

_____

UNIT 4 ✖✖✖✖✖✖✖✖✖✖✖✖✖✖✖✖✖✖✖✖✖✖✖✖✖✖✖✖✖✖✖✖✖✖✖✖✖
Integration of Knowledge and Ideas

4 What can you tell by looking at the picture with passage 2?

    A Microwaves surround the food.

    B Microwave oven food does not taste good.

    C Microwave ovens cook food very quickly.

    D You should never use metal in microwave ovens.

5 List three facts about microwave ovens.

_____

_____

_____

_____

Identifying Connections

RI.2.8

Vocabulary
atmosphere
pilot

Authors must back up or support what they write. They do this with facts. These facts may be from an expert. They may be from a document. A **fact** is a true statement. It can be proven.

Sometimes an author writes about what he thinks or believes. This is his **opinion.** Look for words like *I think, best, worst, everyone, always,* and *never.* This lets you know someone is giving an opinion not a fact. When you read, look for opinions and facts. This helps you know if the author uses reasons to back up or support what he writes.

Think about the points the author makes. How does he support them? Where does he get his facts? Is his information complete? Is his information up to date?

When you are reading, look for connections. Ask yourself why things happen. Ask yourself how they happen, too. It will help you understand what you read.

Think back to the text about microwave ovens. It explained to you the reasons *why* they worked. The author tells you why food made in a microwave does not form a crust. You learned about cause and effect.

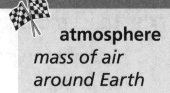

atmosphere
mass of air around Earth

So Why *Is* the Sky Blue?

Have you ever asked, "Why is the sky blue?" Scientists say the answer has to do with light and Earth's atmosphere.

The atmosphere is made up of molecules. These are made of gas. The molecules are mixed with other materials. These other materials can change. For example, after it rains, there can be more water in the air. The atmosphere is thickest near the bottom. It gets thinner as you go higher.

Now, look at the other part of this: light. Light travels in waves. It also travels in a straight line. Sometimes, it bumps into things—like those gas molecules! When light bumps into those, some of it gets absorbed. The molecule then gives off light. This light moves in many directions. This light is the same color that was absorbed.

As light moves, its shorter wavelengths are absorbed. Blue light gets absorbed and then gets scattered. If you look straight up, the sky does look blue. But look at the horizon. (That is the line where the sky looks like it meets Earth!) That light looks pale. That is because the blue light has to travel more to get there. As it travels, it gets scattered.

So now you know: the sky is blue because of the way that light is absorbed. Everyone wants to know why the sky is blue, and now you can tell them!

Which sentence from the report is an opinion?

A Light travels in waves.

B The atmosphere is made up of molecules.

C As light moves, its shorter wavelengths are absorbed.

D Everyone wants to know why the sky is blue, and now you can tell them!

Choices A, B, and C are facts. You can look up these facts in books, which is a good test to see if they are facts or not. The last choice is not a fact. Not everyone wants to know why the sky is blue. And you may or may not be able to explain to anyone. Choice D is the correct answer.

In this text, you can find examples of cause and effect. List one.

_____

_____

_____

Do you remember how to spot cause and effect? Look for words like *so, as a result,* and *because.* Here is a sample answer:

The text tells why the sky near the horizon is pale. It is because the blue light is scattered. This is an example of cause and effect.

Who does the author credit for his facts?

A his parents

B scientists

C himself

D teachers

 The author gives his source in paragraph 1. He says that scientists know why the sky is blue. Choice B is the correct answer. Choices A, C, and D are incorrect. These are not people who studied why the sky is blue.

Paragraph 1 tells you the two main things that work together to make the sky look blue. What are they?

_____

_____

_____

 Think about how things are connected. Here is a sample answer:

Paragraph 1 says that the color of the sky has to do with light and Earth's atmosphere. These are the two main things that work together.

Can you think of anything the author might have used to help the reader to better understand this passage?

_____

_____

_____

 Some nonfiction text is hard to follow. Authors can help the readers understand what they are reading. They can support their facts in different ways. Here is a sample answer:

This passage was hard to follow. We cannot picture the atmosphere. The passage needed some visual aids. This would have helped the reader. A chart might have helped, too.

Are There Different Kinds of Clouds?

pilot
someone who flies an airplane

It would be great to be a pilot! Pilots get to see Earth and the sky from way up high. Clouds look very different to them. But even those of us down on the ground can see—clouds are very interesting!

There are many kinds of clouds. But there are three main types that you will see in the sky. The first type is a "high" cloud, called "cirrus" clouds. These clouds look like party streamers! They are long and wispy. These clouds usually mean fair weather.

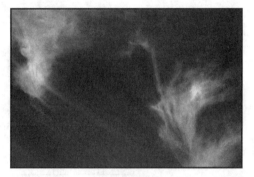

Cirrus clouds

The next common type is called "stratus" clouds. These clouds are gray. When you see them, you know a rain or a drizzle is coming! These clouds look like fog. Because they run together, they can often just look like a gray sky.

Stratus clouds

Now we get to the prettiest cloud: cumulus. They look like cotton balls. These can mean good weather, but if they look like cauliflower and get tall, they can mean bad weather. These clouds that mean bad weather get very tall and large. If you see those, take cover!

So you do not have to be a pilot to see some pretty neat things! Now you know how to spot different clouds!

Cumulus clouds

1 What is the main purpose of this text?

_____

_____

_____

_____

_____

2 What are three facts you learned about cloud types?

Fact 1: _____

_____

Fact 2: _____

_____

Fact 3: _____

_____

3 Which of these is an example of cause and effect?

A It would be great to be a pilot.

B Some clouds look like cotton balls.

C Some clouds can mean that rain is coming.

D Because stratus clouds run together, they look
like gray sky.

UNIT 4 ▚▚▚▚▚▚▚▚▚▚▚▚▚▚▚▚▚▚▚▚▚▚▚▚▚▚▚▚▚▚▚▚▚▚
Integration of Knowledge and Ideas

4 Which of these sentences states an opinion?

    A It would be great to be a pilot.

    B Stratus clouds are gray in color.

    C Cirrus clouds are a type of high cloud.

    D Cumulus clouds can mean either good or bad weather.

5 Read this statement from the passage.

    It would be great to be a pilot.

What reason does the author give to support this statement?

_____

_____

_____

_____

_____

6 How do the photographs support the author's statements?

_____

_____

_____

_____

_____

Comparing and Contrasting

RL.2.9, RI.2.9

Vocabulary
drought
factories
Inuit
landmark

When you read, you probably read different types of texts. **Nonfiction** is the informational text you read to find out about something. Fiction is the stories that you read. **Realistic fiction** is a made-up story that could happen in real life. **Traditional stories** teach a lesson. These include folktales, fairy tales, and fables. **Folktales** are stories about people that teach a lesson about how people act. **Fairy tales** have elements of magic. They might feature giants, wicked witches, or elves. **Fables** are short stories with animals that act and talk like people. A **myth** may explain something about nature. Or, it may explain something about a people's culture.

Do you find that some stories are similar? Do you find that some are different? Many stories can have things in common. The settings might be the same. Sometimes the characters are alike. Think of the story of "Sleeping Beauty." Then think of the story, "Cinderella." They are not about the same thing. But you can find things that are alike in them.

The stories are both about young women. Both fall in love. Neither of them is treated nicely. They have to face challenges. These are the things that are the same. There are also differences. Cinderella is forced to clean her house and perform chores. Sleeping Beauty is put under a spell.

Stories can seem to be very different. But you might find they have things in common, too.

Read two passages. Then answer the questions.

Passage 1

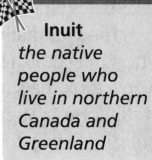

Inuit
the native people who live in northern Canada and Greenland

Crow Brings Daylight

an Inuit myth

Long ago, the Inuit people lived in darkness in Alaska. There was no sun. They could not hunt very well. They could not see wild animals approaching them. They could not see anything! Their friend, Crow, knew about something called daylight. Crow traveled north and south, and he had seen such a thing.

Crow decided to get daylight for the people. He was old, and it would be a hard journey, but he did it. On a sunny day, he set off on his journey. He flew a long, long way to other lands. Finally, he found the spot he was looking for. A young boy was playing outside. In the corner of the garden where the child was, there was a basket. In that basket, there was sunlight! The boy's grandfather owned it.

Crow flew down by the little boy. Crow whispered in the boy's ear: "Tell your grandfather that you are sad because you have no toy to play with! Tell him you want a ball of sunlight!"

Integration of Knowledge and Ideas

The little boy did just that. He cried and said to his grandfather, "Please give me a toy to play with! I want a ball of sunlight!"

The grandfather loved the boy. And he gave him the sunlight. When the grandfather turned away, Crow took the sunlight from the child and flew away with it. He brought it to the Inuit people. He flew that long, long way to bring it to the Inuit people.

The Inuit people were so happy. Crow told them that they would have daylight for six months. He said that then, he would have to fly back and get more. The Inuit people were so happy. They were no longer in darkness.

Passage 2

The Thirsty Crow

a traditional folktale

There was a drought over all the land, but Crow, had to fly a long way to attend his friend's wedding. So Crow took off on his long flight. He flew through the blazing sun; he flew over the desert. He flew, flew, and flew some more. But Crow was not a young bird. He was getting older, and flying was not very easy for him. As the sun beat down on him and the heat got worse, he got very tired.

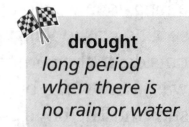

drought
long period when there is no rain or water

Finally, he could not stand it anymore. "I need to have some water!" he cried, "I am too hot, and I must stop flying for awhile!" Crow started looking for a place to stop and rest.

Then, he saw something from up in the sky: a big jar! So, Crow flew down toward the ground. He got to the jar and poked his beak inside, but his beak was too short! Oh, no—what could he do?

How could Crow solve this problem? He saw some rocks and pebbles on the ground, so he picked them up in his beak, one by one. He dropped them slowly into the jar. He was so tired, but he knew it would be worth it!

As Crow dropped the pebbles in the jar, the water level in the jar rose. It got higher and higher. Finally, Crow could take a drink! He drank to his heart's delight. Then he was back on his way. He could not wait to tell all his friends how smart he was! Suddenly, the journey did not seem as long or as tough because he was refreshed!

What is *not* something the two passages have in common?

A The stories are about crows.

B Both crows have to fly a long journey.

C The crows in both stories are getting older.

D Both show how angry people are with the crows.

In passage 1, Crow steals the sun away from a group of people. People should be angry. But they are not. And the Inuit people are very happy. Passage 2 does not show that anyone is angry with Crow. The correct answer is choice D.

What are three things that are different between these stories?

1. _____

_____

2. _____

_____

3. _____

_____

✓ **Think about what is different about the two stories. Here is a sample answer:**

1. Passage 2 is about a drought. Passage 1 is not.
2. Passage 1 is about a crow bringing daylight to the Inuit. Passage 2 is about a crow going to his friend's wedding.
3. In passage 1, the crow helps other people. In passage 2, the crow helps himself not other people.

Informational Text

Authors can tell stories in informational text, too. They might use the same facts. However, they might present them differently. They might use the facts to write a biography, or story of someone's life. They might report the facts only about an event, like in a newspaper story. Just as in stories, you should compare how texts are the same and how they are different.

Guided Practice

Passage 1

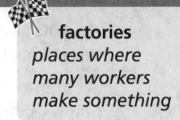

factories
places where many workers make something

Henry Ford: A Biography

Henry Ford was born on July 16, 1863. He was one of six children. He was the oldest child. He grew up on a farm.

At a young age, Ford showed that he did not like farm work. He did like mechanical things. When Ford was 16 years old, he left home. He went to work for a machinist. He had many jobs in the next few years.

Why is this man famous? There are a few reasons. One is that in 1908, he invented the Model-T. This was a car that people could afford to buy. Yet, it was a good car.

Also, he made it easier and faster to build cars. He made assembly lines better. Each worker on an assembly line added, or assembled, a certain part of the car. Ford helped to make assembling a car faster. He brought new ideas about production to factories.

He also started the Ford Motor Company. This happened in 1903. We have probably all heard of that!

Henry Ford did a lot of great things for the auto world. These are just a few of them!

BIG NEWS: Henry Ford's Model-T is Here!

The time is here! And we were first on the scene to report this big event. That is right: the Model-T is out.

Henry Ford had a dream. He wanted to make a car that people could afford. But it also had to be a good car. And he has done it! You see, most cars are made for people with a lot of money. But Ford lowered the cost of this car. Now, more people can buy them.

But who is this Henry Ford? He is the son of farmers. He was born in 1863, and he has always been interested in cars. He knew that farming was not for him. Thank goodness he made the choice to make this car! At $825, it is affordable and great! Because Ford figured out a way to make his assembly line better, the cars are made faster and cheaper.

Sounds like Henry Ford is onto something good! I am sure we will see more from him soon!

What subject do these two passages have in common?

    A the history of American cars

    B Henry Ford and the Model-T

    C the invention of assembly lines

    D how Henry Ford became a farmer

> Both passages are about Henry Ford. Both are about the Model-T. Choice B is the correct answer. The passages are not about all American cars. The passages say that Ford made assembly lines better. They do not say he invented them. Ford did not like farming. Choices A, C, and D are incorrect.

What is one fact from passage 2 that is *not* in passage 1?

    A Ford was born in 1863.

    B The Model-T cost $825.

    C Ford lived on farms for his early life.

    D The Model-T was a car people could afford.

> Choices A, C, and D are facts found in both passages. Only passage 2 tells how much the Model-T cost. The correct answer is choice B.

What is a main difference between these two passages?

_____

_____

_____

✓ **Both passages use the same facts. However, they present them differently. Here is a sample answer:**

> *Passage 1 tells us just about Ford. Passage 2 tells more about the car he made. Passage 1 is written is more like a biography. Passage 2 is more like a news article.*

How do the two passages work together to help you learn more about Henry Ford?

_____

_____

_____

✓ **Think about what facts each passage presents. Think about what you learned from passage 1. Did you learn anything new from passage 2? Here is a sample answer:**

> *Each passage tells something new. We learn about Ford in passage 1. Then in passage 2, we get to better understand why he created the Model-T.*

Passage 1

My Report on Willis Tower

Have you ever been to Willis Tower? You may have been there when it was called something else. It used to be called the Sears Tower. This building is in Chicago.

The tower was not built too long ago. Three men designed the building. The building was started in 1970. It took three years to build it. It was not finished until 1973.

Most people know that this tower is very tall. Just how tall is it? It stands 1,454 feet tall. It is more than one hundred stories high. There are antennas on top of the building. These add two hundred feet to the tower. This makes it look even bigger.

There is also something near the top of the building called Sky Deck. This deck is a glass space that people can stand on and look down at the city from up high.

Many people go to this tower every day. Why? They work there! In fact, about 12,000 people work in the Willis Tower every day.

Sears Tower Changes Name

March 13—

landmark
a well-known object in a certain place

A big change has come to Chicago, Illinois. After being called the Sears Tower since 1973, this tall building will now change its name. The Sears Tower will now be called Willis Tower.

A new company is moving into the tower. They have the right to change the name of the building. In fact, Sears has not been in the building for a long time. However, people will need time to get used to this change. They will probably still use the building's old name when talking about it.

The tower is 110 stories tall. When it was built, it was the tallest building in the world. That was in 1973. Many people know this building. And they know it by its old name. Think of all the people who have to get used to the name change.

There is one more group of people who have to get used to the name change. Who are they? The 12,000 people who work there! They now will call their workplace by a different name.

Some people do not like this new name. This is a real landmark, and those usually do not get new names! This was a big surprise.

1 Which of the following would describe both passages?

   A Both are stories.

   B Both are about the same subject.

   C One is about a person, and one is about a building.

   D Both are about the history of Chicago, Illinois.

2 Which fact is *not* found in both passages?

   A The Willis Tower is in Chicago.

   B Many people work in the Willis Tower.

   C The Sears Tower is now called the Willis Tower.

   D There is a Sky Deck at the very top of the tower.

3 Which of these *best* describes the difference between the two passages?

   A One is fiction and one is not.

   B One is a report and one is a newspaper article.

   C One is a biography and one is a story.

   D One is an interview and one is a report.

4 What is similar and what is different about the way the authors write about their topic?

_____

_____

_____

_____

5 Tell why the name of the tower has changed. Use information from both passages.

_____

_____

_____

_____

UNIT 4 ✖✖✖✖✖✖✖✖✖✖✖✖✖✖✖✖✖✖✖✖✖✖✖✖✖✖✖✖✖
Integration of Knowledge and Ideas

REVIEW

Integration of Knowledge and Ideas

Vocabulary
coyote
locomotive
piston

Read the two passages. Then answer the questions.

Passage 1

coyote
an animal with a long nose and tail; member of wolf family

How the Columbia River Was Formed

One hot day, a coyote was taking a long, long walk. He grew tired, because the heat was really getting to him! As he walked, he made some wishes.

"Oh!" he cried, "I wish that there would be a cloud in the sky!" Why did he want that cloud? Well, because he was hoping for a shadow to keep him cool!

The single cloud came, but that just was not enough! The poor coyote was still so very hot, so he wished again. "Oh!" he cried, "I wish there were many clouds!" And clouds came, making the sky gray.

But still, he was hot, and he began to pant. He needed... what did he need? He needed water, so the coyote wished again. "Oh," he cried, "please send rain! Send a lot of rain!" The sky opened up, and the rain fell down. It poured and it poured…and it poured some more!

It still was not quite enough, so he wished one last time: "Please," he called. "Give me a cold creek to put my feet in!" He just wanted a cool place to put his tired feet. So a creek appeared, and he quickly put his feet in it.

But with all the rain, there was a serious problem— the rain made the creek get bigger, and bigger, and bigger. It just got very big! And it grew to be so large that it was too big to be a creek. It became—a river! And that is how the Columbia River was formed—at least that is what the old story says.

Passage 2

Why Possum Has a Pouch

One evening, Possum was walking with her babies. She was enjoying the sunset, and so were her little ones. Suddenly, a big bat came down from the sky. He swooped in so fast that the possums hardly saw him! With no warning, he scooped up the babies and flew away with them.

Possum was upset, and she cried out for help. Rabbit came to help her first. "Oh, Rabbit," she said, "I need to get my babies back!"

"Okay!" Rabbit replied, "I can do that." So off he went. Possum waited… and then, Rabbit came back. "I am sorry," he said, "but I could not get them!"

So Possum cried out again, and this time, Wolf came along to help her. But he had the same luck as Rabbit! What in the world was going on?

Then an old turtle came walking down the road. "Oh, please, Turtle," said Possum. "I am desperate. I need help! Please get my babies back from that evil bat!"

Turtle was very wise. In fact, he had a few magic tricks up his sleeve. So he went for the bat. Of course, the tricky bat had set out many obstacles for him! But he got through them.

When Turtle got back to Possum, he spoke to her. "Here are your babies," he said. Then he cast a magic spell. "Look down," he said.

Possum looked down to find that she had a pouch in her belly now! "Your babies can ride in there," said Turtle. "They will stay safe in your pouch. Keep them in there until they are old enough to take better care of themselves!" That is how the legend says that possums got their pouches.

1 Both of these stories feature _____.

   A people

   B animals

   C rivers

   D sunsets

2 What is one difference between Coyote in passage 1 and Possum in passage 2?

   A Coyote asks for help.

   B Coyote has a problem.

   C Possum gets help.

   D Possum has little babies.

3 What does the picture in passage 2 help you understand?

   A what is in the pouch

   B why the pouch was made

   C what the pouch looks like

   D why the babies stay there

4 Tell how Coyote and Possum are the same.

_____

_____

_____

_____

Passage 1

The Invention of Trains

Ding, ding, ding! Have you ever been stuck at a railroad crossing? You have probably seen trains before. Do you know how old they are?

The first train, or locomotive, was made in 1804. It was powered by steam. The steam came from burning wood or coal, which heated water to make steam. The steam went into a cylinder with a piston. The piston was connected with a rod to the wheels. When the piston moved, it moved the wheels.

However, steam was not the best way to run trains. The trains needed lots of wood or coal to make steam. In the 1890s, a man with the last name Diesel invented the diesel train. The diesel engine is like the engine that runs a car. Diesel engines can be used in many things. They can power cars, trucks, and tractors. These diesel trains are what we see today.

The diesel trains were cleaner than steam. They did not need fuel as often. They did not need repairs as often. They were also more powerful. It would take two steam engines to do the work of one diesel engine!

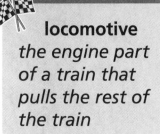

locomotive
the engine part of a train that pulls the rest of the train

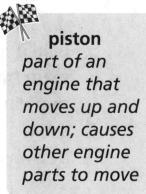

piston
part of an engine that moves up and down; causes other engine parts to move

Steam Train

The History of the Railroad

Railroads are a major part of our history.

Railroads began to be used in the 1820s. They helped people get from place to place faster. Before railroads, travel was very slow. People had to walk. Or, they had to ride a horse or wagon. The railroads brought people together. People could ship goods across the land. Railroads helped the country grow.

The time between the 1880s and the 1920s was called the railroad's golden age. Trains were used as the main transportation. After the car and airplane became popular, railroads were not used as much. Trains are still a good form of public transportation. People are beginning to use them more.

At first, trains were powered by steam. It took a long time for that to change. Then diesel trains came along. These trains were cleaner. They had more power. They needed fewer repairs. Now, a newer train is used in other countries. This train runs by electromagnetics. It is called a maglev train. Some people want to build maglev trains in this country. No matter what powers them, trains have helped shape our country. We love our trains. They are a big part of history.

Diesel Train

Maglev Train

UNIT 4
Integration of Knowledge and Ideas

5 Which of these statements in passage 2 is an opinion?

    A Before trains, travel was very slow.

    B Railroads began to be used in the 1820s.

    C Trains are a good form of public transportation.

    D They helped people get from place to place faster.

6 Both passages give reasons for diesel being better than steam. Which of these reasons was given in both passages?

    A Diesel is cleaner than steam.

    B Diesel looks better than steam.

    C Diesel costs much more than steam.

    D Diesel engines power cars and tractors.

7 How do the pictures help you understand the passages?

    A They show how trains work.

    B They show why trains are better than cars.

    C They show what the different trains look like.

    D They show why there were not many trains at first.

8 Give an example of a fact from passage 1. How do you know it is *not* an opinion?

_____

_____

_____

_____

_____

9 How are the two passages similar?

_____

_____

_____

_____

_____

10 How are the passages different?

_____

_____

_____

_____

_____

UNIT 4 ✖✖✖✖✖✖✖✖✖✖✖✖✖✖✖✖✖✖✖✖✖✖✖✖✖✖ **UNIT** ✖✖✖✖✖
Integration of Knowledge and Ideas

PRACTICE TEST

scrap
very small piece

Read the story. Then answer the questions.

The Old Woman Who Became a Woodpecker

a legend of the Northland

Far up north, winter days are short, and nights are very long. Reindeer pull heavy sleds. Children look like bear cubs in their funny, furry clothes. It was there, long ago, that a good traveler walked along the snowy roads.

One day, the traveler came to a cottage. He looked in and saw a little old woman making cakes and baking them on the hearth. The good traveler had not eaten for days. He went to her door to ask the woman if she would give him a cake. Just one small cake would end his hunger.

The little old woman made a very small cake. She placed it on the hearth to bake. Then she looked at it and thought, "That is a big cake. It is much too big for me to give away to a stranger."

Then the little old woman made another cake. It was much smaller. She laid it on the hearth to bake. But when she turned it over, it looked too good to give away.

Then the little old woman took just a tiny scrap of dough. She rolled it out and rolled it out. She made it as thin as could be. But when it was done, it was one of the nicest cakes she had made. She told the man, "My cakes are just too good to give away."

The good traveler grew angry. He was so very, very hungry. "You are greedy. You do not deserve food, shelter, and a warm fire. From now on, you shall build like a bird builds a nest. You will eat only nuts and berries. And all day long, you will drill and drill in the bark of trees."

As soon as the good traveler said these words, the little old woman went straight up the chimney. When she flew out at the top, her feathers were as black as coal. Her head was red in shame. She had changed into a red-headed woodpecker!

Now every boy and girl can see her in the woods. Her bright head makes her easy to find. She lives in the trees. She hunts nuts and berries for food. She drills and drills in the bark of trees.

1 The setting is described at the beginning. Where does the story take place?

   A a warm, sunny place

   B a hot, wet, rainy place

   C a future place with spaceships

   D a cold, snowy place with long nights

2 What is the author's purpose in writing this story?

   A to persuade the reader not to speak to strangers

   B to explain why woodpeckers are found up north

   C to tell the reader how to make really good cakes

   D to show what can happen to greedy people

3 Which sentence said by the little old woman shows that she is greedy?

   A That is a big cake.

   B You will eat only nuts and berries.

   C My cakes are just too good to give away.

   D You do not deserve food, shelter, and a warm fire.

4 Near the end of the story, what does the reader learn about the good traveler?

   A He likes cake.

   B He has special powers.

   C He is really, really hungry.

   D He is a red-headed woodpecker.

5 At the end of the story, why was the little old woman turned into a red-headed woodpecker?

   A so the good traveler could live in her house and eat all her cakes

   B so she would be greedy and uncaring to strangers who come to her door

   C so she would never again make cakes, bake them on her hearth, and put them on her shelf

   D so she would know what it is like to live outdoors in the winter cold and have to hunt for food

6 Which word could be used instead of the word <u>hearth</u> in paragraph 2?

A coal

B wood

C floor

D fireplace

7 Why does the man ask the woman for a cake?

A He smells the cakes baking.

B He has not eaten for days.

C He has been walking in the snow

D He knows she has plenty of cakes.

8 What is the theme of this story?

_____

_____

_____

_____

_____

http://www.birdwatchingfun.com

Welcome   Bird Feeders   Bird Houses   Bird Food Recipes   Bird Photography

Bird Watching is Family Fun

Everyone likes being outdoors. Bird watching is a great way to be outdoors all year long. It makes us more aware of the natural world around us. Bird watching brings nature to life.

It is easy to start bird watching. You do not need to know a lot about birds. You can watch birds from almost anywhere. It does not cost much. You need a bird field guide from the library or bookstore.

You can watch the birds in your own backyard. Hang up a bird feeder to attract wild birds. Build a simple platform feeder from a few pieces of wood. Or, create a suet feeder from a pinecone covered in peanut butter and rolled in birdseed. Make your own wild bird food and watch the birds enjoy it.

What kinds of birds will come to your feeder? How many? Use a field guide to learn their names. Start a bird-watching journal. Keep notes and write down the birds you see each day. Take pictures and start a photo album.

Bird watching is a hobby for the whole family. It brings us together. Plan a day trip to look for birds in their natural habitat. Make bird watching part of your family vacation. No matter where you travel, you will find birds. Watching wild birds can grow into a lifelong love for nature.

Bird watching is a hobby the whole family can enjoy.

Favorite Backyard Birds
Click on the icon below to send us your favorite backyard bird photo.

9 Which describes the structure of this text?

    A a web page

    B a magazine article

    C a letter

    D a poem

10 Which text feature on the page is most helpful to find out where to send your bird photo?

    A icon

    B photo

    C menu

    D caption

11 What is the author's purpose for writing this passage?

    A to entertain with stories about birds

    B to explain more about bird watching

    C to persuade the reader to take up a hobby

    D to describe the different types of birds

12 Use the text and the illustration to answer this question. What type of bird feeder are the birds using?

_____

_____

_____

_____

_____

Read the passage. Then answer the questions.

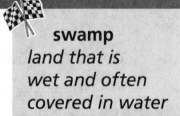

swamp
land that is wet and often covered in water

Black Bears

Black bears are the bears most often found in North America. Most often, they live in forests. Some black bears live in the mountains or near swamps.

There are some things you might not know about black bears. Did you know that black bears are amazing tree climbers? They have strong feet and nails to help them. There is another thing you may not know. Black bears not just black. Some are gray, brown, or even white.

Black bears usually eat grass, roots, berries, and bugs. You may have also seen pictures of them eating fish and other small animals. Maybe you have seen them eating garbage near your campsite? Never feed the bears! They are dangerous and can hurt you.

During the winter months, bears hibernate. They sleep in their dens living off the body fat they have built up in the summer and fall. Their dens may be in caves, tree holes, or piles of brush.

There are many facts about black bears you may not know. They can grow to be five or six feet long. They can weigh between 200 and 600 pounds. Black bears live to be about 20 years old.

Where else can you look to learn more about black bears?

13 Which of these is the topic of paragraph 4?

   A Bears like to sleep.

   B Bears live in dens.

   C Bears go to sleep during the winter.

   D Bears like to eat a lot during the year.

14 According to the article, black bears are mostly found in _____.

   A South America

   B North America

   C Central America

   D American islands

15 Why is it important to never feed bears?

   A They might start liking human food.

   B They will not get enough food for the winter.

   C They are very dangerous and can hurt people.

   D They will get very ill if they eat the food we eat.

16 What is the author's purpose in writing this passage?

A to explain

B to persuade

C to entertain

D to describe

17 How does the photograph support a point that the author makes in the passage?

_____

_____

_____

_____

_____

Read the poem. Then answer the questions.

The Naughty Little Robin
by Phoebe Cary

1 Once there was a robin,
2 Lived outside the door;
3 Who wanted to go inside
4 And hop upon the floor.

5 "No, no," said the mother,
6 "You must stay with me;
7 Little birds are safest,
8 Sitting in a tree."

9 "I don't care," said Robin,
10 And gave his tail a fling;
11 "I don't think the old folks
12 Know quite everything."

13 Down he flew and Kitty seized[1] him
14 Before he had time to blink,
15 "Oh!" he cried, "I'm sorry,
16 But I just didn't think."

18 What is the text structure used here?

A words and sentences

B sentences and paragraphs

C lines and stanzas

D paragraphs and chapters

19 From whose point of view is this poem told?

A the kitty

B the little robin

C the mother robin

D an outside narrator

20 Which words rhyme in stanza 4?

A flew and before

B him and sorry

C blink and think

D Kitty and seized

---

[1]**seized:** grabbed

21 At the end of the poem, what did the little robin say to let his mother know that he had been wrong?

A I don't care!

B Oh, I'm sorry. I just didn't think.

C Little birds are safest sitting in a tree.

D I don't think the old folks know everything.

Read the two passages. Then answer the questions.

Passage 1

chuckled
laughed

Rabbit Earns a Dollar a Minute

Fox decided one day that he would grow himself some peas. So he set out to do just that. He watched his garden and the peas grew well. But then tricky Rabbit decided that he wanted to get some of those peas! Rabbit started sneaking into the garden to steal the peas.

Fox grew wise to this pesky trick. So he set a trap! He just knew that Rabbit was behind the pea-theft! He rigged a rope to trap Rabbit. When Rabbit stepped on the rope, he would be pulled up into a tree!

Rabbit went to steal peas the next day. Sure enough, he was pulled up into a tree! But, that tricky Rabbit, he always had a plan. He watched for Bear to come walking down the road. When Bear finally arrived, Rabbit called out to him. "Hey, Bear!" he said. Look at me! I am earning a dollar a minute from Fox!"

"How?" cried Bear. This was good money. He was very excited to hear about it!

"Well," Rabbit lied, "he assured me that if I act like a scarecrow and watch over his pea garden, he would pay me that dollar a minute!"

Bear was excited. He really wanted to give this a try. "Mind if I give this scarecrow thing a try?" he asked.

"Be my guest!" said Rabbit. Bear helped Rabbit down from the tree. He untied the rope, and he tied himself in. Bear then flew up to the top of the tree, just as Rabbit had.

Rabbit chuckled to himself. He had outsmarted Fox and Bear—and he was still going to eat those peas.

Passage 2

Turtle Tricks the Fox

Rabbit was known for being tricky. He decided one day to become friends with Turtle, and the two of them really hit it off. The two of them grew very fond of tricking Fox. Well, Fox was not fond of this! He did not appreciate it at all. He took every opportunity to chase after both Rabbit and Turtle.

Now Fox never could catch Rabbit—but Turtle was slow. He could come close to catching Turtle! One day when Turtle was walking down the road, Fox caught him by the tail.

He cried out to Turtle: "Well, what will you do now? I have finally caught you!"

What Fox did not know was that Turtle had a plan. "Please!" Turtle said. "Please do not throw me in the pond! Anything but the pond! I will drown!"

"Ah-ha!" said Fox slyly. "You should not have said anything. For now I will throw you in the pond!"

Turtle pretended to be upset. Then Fox threw him into the pond. Turtle disappeared.

Then Fox realized something. Turtle lived in the pond! He loved the pond! He would not drown at all!

Fox dove into the river to get Turtle. But as he dove he heard something. Turtle was laughing! Fox could not swim well. And Turtle was swimming toward shore laughing.

22 What do Rabbit in passage 1 and Turtle in passage 2 have in common?

   A They like to play games.

   B They like to play tricks on Fox.

   C They both can swim very well.

   D They each take care of their families.

23 What is different about the two main animals in these stories?

A Rabbit is fast; Turtle is slow.

B Rabbit tells a lie to Fox; Turtle does not.

C Rabbit eats a lot of peas; Turtle eats Fox.

D Rabbit likes Fox; Turtle does not like Fox.

24 What does the illustration in passage 2 show you? How does it help you better understand the story?

_____

_____

_____

_____

_____

25 Read the sentence from passage 2.

"Ah-ha!" said Fox slyly.

What word might be used in place of <u>slyly</u> that would keep the same meaning?

A kindly

B hastily

C cleverly

D honestly

Passage 1

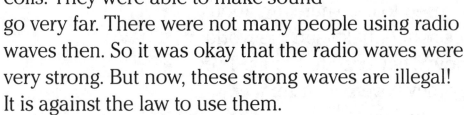

illegal
not allowed

How Radios Work

Radios are a part of our history. Before TV, people used to listen to them all the time. Radios use waves to make sound. They can let us hear music, the news, and more. These waves can make sound travel across many miles.

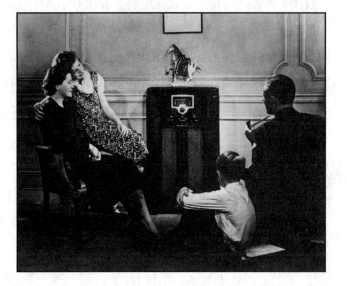

When the first sound machines were used, the things that helped the sound move were called spark coils. They were able to make sound go very far. There were not many people using radio waves then. So it was okay that the radio waves were very strong. But now, these strong waves are illegal! It is against the law to use them.

So what do we use now? Radios now use something called sine waves to make sound move. A transmitter is what sends the sound. A receiver is what picks up the sound. Both use an antenna to give off or pick up the sound.

The same waves that bring you the sound of radio also bring other sounds. Baby monitors also use these waves. So do police scanners. Each of these uses a different signal.

These waves are really neat. They travel fast. You cannot see them. But they carry sound to your car radio, your house radio, and any other that you can think of! And they are safe.

Passage 2

The Invention of the Radio

Do you listen to the radio? Did you know that they have been around for a long time? In fact, it was almost the 1900s when a man sent these signals for the first time. The signals, or waves, could only travel for about one mile at that time. They could not go far.

People do not agree about who first made this machine. Many say it was a man named Marconi. He is the one who sent those first signals. Others say that it was their idea. A man named Bose said that he made it first. Most people think a man named Tesla invented it.

Today, there are thousands of radio stations! That is a lot more than there used to be. There are about two billion of these little sound makers in the world. Radios look different now. They used to be big. They looked like boxes. Now they have gotten smaller. They can even fit in your pocket!

26 How are these two passages alike?

_____

_____

_____

_____

_____

27 How are these two passages different?

_____

_____

_____

_____

_____

28 What does the picture in passage 1 help you
understand about the text?

_____

_____

_____

_____

_____

29 Why were radios very important when they were
first made?

  A People liked to listen to music.

  B Because no one knows who created the radio.

  C People used it to get the news, because there
  was no TV.

  D Radios were not very important when they were
  first made.

30 List three facts used in passage 1.

_____

_____

_____

_____

_____

GLOSSARY

A

Aardvark an animal with a long, pointed nose

Allergic getting sick when around animal hair, plants, or foods that do not bother other people

Alliteration repeated beginning sounds of words

Antonyms words with an opposite meaning

Astray not looking straight ahead; looking around

Atmosphere mass of air around Earth

C

Chuckled laughed

Coyote an animal with a long nose and tail; member of wolf family

Crust hard outside coating

Curds and Whey cheese, like cottage cheese

Customers people who buy something

D

Decorations items put around the house for holidays

Directed show or explain how to do something

Dismay unhappy, or upset

Dreary sad and dull

Drought long period when there is no rain or water

E

Enormous	very large
Exercise	physical activity
Extinct	animal that does not live any more

F

Fact	a statement or information that can be proven
Factories	places where many workers make something
Frustrated	upset

H

Hibernation	stage of rest for some animals during winter
Honest	tells the truth
Hyperbole	exaggerated statement for effect

I

Illegal	not allowed
Illustrator	someone who creates the pictures in a book
Intrigued	interested
Inuit	the native people who live in northern Canada and Greenland

K

Kernels	the part of the corn cob that is eaten
Key Words	list of important words in a text

L

Landmark	a well-known object in a certain place
Lawyer	a person who practices or studies law
Locomotive	the engine part of a train that pulls the rest of the train

 **Mammal** — warm-blooded animal that gives birth to live young

Medicine — anything used to treat an injury or illness

Metaphor — type of figurative language that compares two unlike things but does not use *like* or *as*

Onomatopoeia — words that sound like what they mean

Opinion — something that someone believes or thinks

Pardon — to let go or excuse

Personification — giving human characteristics to a concept or inanimate object

Pilot — someone who flies an airplane

Piston — part of an engine that moves up and down; causes other engine parts to move

Point of view — who is telling the story

   first-person — the main character is telling the story; uses first person pronouns *I* and *we*

   third-person — an outside narrator or character in a story is telling the story; uses third-person pronouns *he, she,* and *they*

Poison — something that can cause illness or death when eaten

Prefix — part of a word added to beginning of another word that changes the meaning of the word

President — head of the United States

Propel — to push up

R — **Rescue**   saves

Rhyme   repeated sounds at the ends of words

Rhythm   pattern of stressed and unstressed beats in a line of poetry

Rotate   to spin

S — **Scrap**   very small piece

Seized   grabbed

Settlers   people who settle in an area; colonists

Shabby   not well kept

Simile   type of figurative language that compares two unlike things using *as* or *like*

Spare   to save

Stanza   a group of lines within a poem

Startled   surprised

Storm Surge   large waves from a hurricane

Suffix   part of a word added to the end of another word that changes the meaning of the word

Swamp   land that is wet and often covered in water

Synonyms   words that have a similar meaning

T — **Toxic**   affected by or caused by something that is poisonous

Trill   vibrating sound like the warbling song of a bird

Tuffet   stool